SACRAMENTO PUBLIC LIBRARY
828 "I" STREET
SACRAMENTO, CA 95814
12/2010

The
Boxer
Handbook

Joan Hustace Walker

D0009638

BARRON'S

Acknowledgments

This book could not have been written without the tremendous support and tireless help of many Boxer fanciers in both Germany and the United States. I would like to express my deepest appreciation to German Boxer fanciers Rosi Westphal, Willibald Wendel, and the Rausch family, Heinrich Mörtl, the many enthusiastic members of the Wetzlar, Germany training club, and the Boxer Klub e.v. Sitz München. Among the American Boxer fanciers, I would like to extend a special thank you to Tracy Hendrickson, the late Wendy Wallner, D.V.M., Calvin Gruver, Cathy Markos, Ann Gilbert, Molly Bachman, and Mary Stocker. And, of course, my gratitude to my husband, Randy, and my children, Eric and Grace, for their unwavering support during the researching and writing of this book, and for their mutual love of dogs.

Photo Credits

Norvia Behling: page 81; Seth Casteel: pages 20, 21, 83, 108, 122, 162; Kent Dannen: page 50; Tracy Hendrickson: pages vi, 3, 10, 15, 17, 26, 27, 28, 45, 47, 62, 72, 76, 92, 98, 101, 105, 106, 110, 113, 116, 121, 129, 130, 169, 171, 179, 180, 183, 184, 188; Cathy Hubert: pages 4, 7, 16, 18, 68, 97, 125; Karen Hudson: 33, 36, 64, 144, 149; Jeanmfogle.com: pages 40, 114, 127, 154, 170, 181; Daniel Johnson: pages 8, 29, 71, 91, 115, 161; Paulette Johnson: pages 53, 87, 88, 138, 140, 164; Pets by Paulette: page 39; Shutterstock: pages 49, 55, 56, 58, 90, 93, 94, 185, 195, 198; Kira Stackhouse: pages 65, 119, 143, 178; Connie Summers: pages 12, 23, 30, 34, 37, 43, 66, 75, 78, 80, 85, 102, 131, 132, 135, 136, 146, 150, 157, 159, 172, 173, 175.

©Copyright 2010, 2000 by Joan Hustace Walker

All rights reserved.
No part of this book may be reproduced in any form or by any means without the written permission of the copyright owner.

All inquiries should be addressed to:
Barron's Educational Series, Inc.
250 Wireless Boulevard
Hauppauge, New York 11788
www.barronseduc.com

ISBN-13: 978-0-7641-4342-7
ISBN-10: 0-7641-4342-5

Library of Congress Control Number: 2010924949

Printed in China

9 8 7 6 5 4 3 2 1

About the Author

Joan Hustace Walker has been writing professionally since 1984. She is a member of the Authors Guild, the American Society of Journalists and Authors, the Dog Writers Association of America, and the Cat Writers Association. Walker has written more than 18 books and has had hundreds of articles published by a variety of national and international magazines, as well as local and regional newspapers. Her work has received more than 30 national nominations and awards, including six Maxwell Awards from the Dog Writers Association of America.

Cover Credits

Seth Casteel: front cover (top right); Cheryl Ertelt: back cover (top right); Karen Hudson: front cover (bottom right), spine; Daniel Johnson: front cover (top left); Shutterstock: front cover (bottom left), back cover (bottom left).

Important Note

This pet handbook gives advice to the reader about buying and caring for a new dog. The author and publisher consider it important to point out that the advice given in the book applies to normally developed puppies or adult dogs, obtained from recognized dog breeders or adoption shelters, dogs that have been examined and are in excellent health with good temperament.

Anyone who adopts a grown dog should be aware that the animal has already formed its basic knowledge of human beings and their customs. The new owner should watch the animal carefully, especially its attitude and behavior toward humans. If possible, the new owner should meet the former owners before adopting the dog. If the dog is adopted from a shelter, the new owner should make an effort to obtain information about the dog's background, personality, and peculiarities. Dogs that come from abusive homes or from homes in which they have been treated abnormally may react to handling in an unnatural manner, and may have a tendency to snap or bite. Dogs with this nature should only be adopted by people who have had experience with such dogs.

Caution is further advised in the association of children with dogs, both puppies and adults, and in meeting other dogs, whether on or off lead.

Well-behaved and carefully supervised dogs may cause damage to someone else's property or cause accidents. It is therefore in the owner's interest to be adequately insured against such eventualities, and we strongly urge all dog owners to purchase a liability policy that covers their dog.

Contents

Chapter One

History of the Boxer

The Boxer originated in southern Germany more than 100 years ago. Today, the Boxer has become one of the best loved and most popular breeds, not only in his homeland, but in many other areas of the world, as well—and for good reason. In addition to cutting a striking image with his well-muscled physique, classic, chiseled head, and smooth, glossy coat, the Boxer is extremely versatile.

Boxers are wonderful family dogs as well as keen competitors in both show and performance events. The Boxer is just as comfortable playing endless games of catch (or catch me!) with the kids in the backyard as he is striking a pose in the show ring or flying through suspended tires in agility competitions. Many Boxers still have what it takes to be superlative Schutzhund dogs—tracking, obedience, and protection work— and continue to be used today in drug detection, search and rescue, and even police work. But above all, the Boxer is a loyal and loving companion who truly lives to please his owner.

Early History

The friendly, congenial Boxer of today has his origins in a now-extinct hunting breed that dates back to the Middle Ages, the Brabanter Bullenbeisser. This strong, agile dog is said to have originated in Brabant, Belgium, and was used by noblemen to hunt wild boars in southern Germany. To the north and in Poland, a much larger bull-baiting dog was being used, called the Danziger Bullenbeisser. Historical accounts of the Brabanter Bullenbeisser note that the dog was dark in color, usually fawn or brindle with a black mask. The dog also had an undershot jaw so that it could hold onto the boar and still breathe through its nose. It is said that the Brabanter Bullenbeisser tackled game from the back and grabbed the animal by its neck or back, similar to the manner in which Boxers were originally trained in early protection work. The ears of the Brabanter Bullenbeisser were cropped closely in order to prevent the boar from ripping an ear, a potentially bloody and serious injury.

After the Napoleonic wars, the aristocracy who owned packs of Brabanter Bullenbeissers were dispersed. The talented dog, however, quickly found a new job as the local butcher or cattle dealer's dog. In this position, the smaller Bullenbeisser was used to hold and help control an animal for the butcher or cattle dealer. By the 1800s the Bullenbeisser was no longer a dog of the elite, but was now a dog of the working class. When not at work, the breed was a family pet and guardian of the home, captivating an increasing number of Germans.

It is thought that around 1830 an early form of the English Bulldog, one much taller and with a much smaller head than today's show dogs, was interbred with the Brabanter Bullenbeisser. This crossing makes sense, since the English Bulldog was bred for the same purposes as the Bullenbeisser. This crossing of the two breeds introduced white and particolored or "check" dogs, and was the foundation of the Boxer breed as it is known today.

Development of the Breed

The German Boxer Klub relates that the first reference to the Boxer as a breed occurred as early as 1860 or 1870. The reason for giving a German breed an English name never has been totally understood, though some have theorized that the name stems from the dog's unique use of his forelegs when fighting. Boxers today still display this trait and will try to wrap their strong forelegs around the Schutzhund "helper" (bad guy) when commanded to attack.

In 1895 the German Boxer Klub (Boxer-Klub e.v. Sitz München) was formed in Munich, Germany. The newly formed club developed a breed standard to better define what a Boxer should look like, since in the early days there was much variety in type and style. A dog show was held soon thereafter, and efforts to breed a Boxer conforming to the idealized standard began in earnest.

It is interesting to note that historical photos show that a large number—if not a majority—of early Boxers were either white in color or predominantly white with patches of color. In 1925 white and "check" Boxers were declared unacceptable in Germany for registration and showing. One theory regarding this change in heart over acceptable and disqualifying colors is that the decision was influenced by Boxer breeders—and perhaps government officials—to maximize the number of Boxers eligible for police and military service. To put it simply, white Boxers could be seen at night and dark Boxers could not. If the numbers of solid or near solid fawn and brindle dogs could be increased, and the numbers of white Boxers decreased, the German police and military forces would have more Boxers eligible for service.

A look at historical photos of the Boxers registered in the first decade of the breed shows a dog that looks quite different from today's highly refined breed. Early Boxers were thicker in build, longer in body, and coarser in the head. Within 20 years, however, the outline of today's Boxer began to emerge. With the herculean efforts of German breeders such as Friederun Stockmann (1891–1972) and her kennels, "vom Dom" (translated as "from the Cathedral"), Germany was able to quickly develop uniformity within the breed and a dog that more closely conformed to the breed standard, or perfection.

However, it wasn't easy for Stockmann and other devoted Boxer breeders to accomplish this task. During World War I, Stockmann relates in her book, *My Life with Boxers,* that there was a severe food shortage and it was a constant hardship to feed her dogs. She describes searching for scraps to feed them by digging through garbage cans at the military barracks. She once bicycled more than 10 miles to pick up a half bucket of intestines. Other times she was forced to do the unspeakable: Feed dog meat to her very own dogs. When her bicycle tires wore out, she wrote that she used braided feathers.

Though the Boxers working on the front lines ate better than those left behind, the Boxers at home were in many ways the lucky ones. Working Boxers suffered heavy casualties during WWI. Keep in mind that these dogs included some of Germany's very best Boxers from the finest kennels. Stockmann relates in her book that her husband, Philip, who organized the training and placement of

Boxers as war dogs, took 10 dogs with him and returned with only one. The ravages of war were devastating to Germany's supply of Boxers.

The First World War was followed by a period of tremendous inflation and a bad situation became even worse. Food was again in extreme shortage. Also, Boxers that had survived WWI were often sterile. Of the litters that were born, there was a high mortality rate. Just when German breeders were beginning to recover, they would be hit with another extreme setback. When it became clear that a second world war was imminent, Stockmann wrote that many breeders sold and shipped their Boxers out of the country. A large number of dogs were reportedly killed in advance of any suffering.

When WWII did finally break out, it was equally as devastating to German Boxer breeders and their dogs as World War I. Frau Stockmann wrote that dogs were tested and qualified for their abilities to perform as war dogs and then were whisked off, never to be seen again, leaving owners to guess at their beloved dogs' fates. Only dogs that had passed the rigorous tests in obedience, tracking, messenger, and protection work were given a sort of meal ticket that allowed these Boxers to receive food. With severe food shortages everywhere, this was a particularly important allowance to have for the dogs. It also meant that Boxer breeders worked very hard to make sure all their dogs passed the tests in order to have access to food.

It wasn't until years after the conclusion of World War II that the Boxer in Germany would regain his foothold and continue his long tradition of excellence.

Service to Mankind

As mentioned earlier, the Boxer's ancestors served their masters by hunting wild boar and later working as butchers' dogs. When the war began in Germany, the Boxer's duties took another turn.

During World War I, Boxers were part of the 50,000 dogs that were trained and combat-ready in Germany. During the course of the war, Boxers were employed in a variety of jobs. Some Boxers served as guards, making sure that while standing in line, POWs weren't able to pass information to civilians. Boxers were also used to halt smuggling into and out of the country and on the front lines to detect the enemy, alerting the handler by growling softly. Still others were trained to attack anyone who shot at their handlers.

Messenger dogs, or couriers, were trained to carry messages in tubes on their collars. The dogs had to be able to travel long distances quietly and without barking while in enemy fire. In a related duty, war dogs were also called upon to carry a roll of telephone or telegraph wire to link one point to another. Boxers assigned to patrol work were surefooted and became noted for their uncanny ability to lead their handlers along routes even when the handlers did not know their way.

Ambulance Dogs

One of the most interesting facets of war work was the medic or ambulance dog. During World War I, Boxers were trained to seek out wounded soldiers, bite off the soldier's tag, and return to lead a medic to the soldier. One Boxer that was trained to perform this duty saved so many lives during the war that she was awarded

My Life with Boxers

Reprints of Friederun von Miram-Stockmann's book *Ein Leben mit Boxern (My Life with Boxers)* are available. Currently, the only version is a reprint of the 3rd edition of the original book (Gollwitzer: 2004). Unfortunately for those who are searching for an English translation, this book is written in German. (For those who *do* read German, the book is available online.) It is possible, however, for those seeking an English version of this book to find used copies of the most recent English translation by Calvin D. Gruver (Classic Pet Books: 1998). This English edition contains not only a clear translation of the original German text, but also an expanded collection of Frau Stockmann's original line drawings.

This book chronicles Stockmann's life with her Boxers and the almost insurmountable hardships she and her Boxers survived.

Germany's highest honor, the Iron Cross. The female Boxer, Matthias vom Westen, was one of the Stockmann's dogs; however, the German Boxer Klub's records are unclear as to whether Philip Stockmann himself handled the dog, or if it was another soldier. Matthias' war effort is a tribute to this breed's bravery and dedication to the task at hand under the most frightening conditions.

U.S. War Dogs

The Boxer also had an influence in the war effort on the other side of the ocean. Although the United States did not have a canine corps (they were lucky if they were able to use French, Belgian, and English war dogs), there is one American dog that was promoted to "honorary sergeant" by the U.S. Army for his service during the war. Stubby, so named for his docked tail, reportedly was a homeless Boxer or Boxer-cross (there may have been a Bull Terrier involved, according to companion animal historian and author Mary Elizabeth Thurston in *The Lost History of the Canine Race*).

Stubby is credited with saving his regiment many times by alerting the men to incoming mortar shells. A fine sense of smell also enabled Stubby to warn the men of mustard gas and he barked furiously until they put on their gas masks. (Stubby had his own gas mask that the regiment had crafted just for the dog.) Though Stubby perhaps was not a purebred Boxer, he certainly possessed the valiant heart of this breed.

After World War I, the United States developed a K9 Corps that included Boxers in its initial 32 breeds advocated for military work. The Boxer was also showcased in Dogs for Defense promotional posters in which a soldier and his Boxer were illustrated along with the words: "War Dogs for Our Armed Forces. Give Dogs and Dollars to Dogs for Defense." By the end of World War II, Boxers had served valiantly; however, German Shepherd dogs had become the dog of choice.

After World War I in Germany

Specific breeds of dogs were approved for police and military work in Germany. Interestingly, even though the Boxer reportedly was the first breed of dog used in the war, it was not approved for police and military service until 1921. The seven breeds that were first approved for police and military service were the Airedale, Boxer, Doberman Pinscher, German Shepherd, Giant Schnauzer, Hovawart, and Rottweiler. The Belgian Malinois and Bouvier were added at a later date; other breeds such as the Labrador Retriever and some mixed breeds were used by Customs as narcotics search dogs.

In December 1940, the German government required that all potential military dogs were to be tested for their ability to perform this type of work. Those dogs that passed would be registered for future service and would be allowed to breed in the meantime. Dogs that passed the test were also issued a rationing card for dog food. Records show that 32 percent of all Boxers tested passed. The only breed to have a higher passing percentage was the Airedale Terrier with 33 percent.

Stockmann relates that at the conclusion of World War II, German Shepherd dogs became the most popular dog of the military. She credits this preference to the fact that German Shepherds have a thick coat and can survive in much harsher weather than the smooth-coated Boxer. She also noted that the German Shepherd was easier to train than the Boxer and didn't require as experienced a handler.

Service Work Today

The Boxer today remains a top choice in many areas of service work. It is still an accepted breed for police work in Germany, and despite the common saying that "in the time it takes to train one Boxer, you can train two German Shepherds," Boxers are still trained from time to time as police dogs. They are also used quite successfully as search and rescue dogs for the Red Cross.

In the United States, Boxers are used as drug detection dogs and as search and rescue (SAR) dogs. In Wisconsin, Cathy and George Markos (Bachbett Boxers) have been training working Boxers as police K9s for more than a decade. Their Boxers currently are employed as full-time police K9s in both Wisconsin and Iowa, with requests for additional Boxer police K9s coming in

from all over the country. These working Boxers are either trained for drug detection or are dual trained: drug detection *and* patrol/tracking. And they're *good*. Recently, dual-purpose K9 "Cliff," a Boxer working with the La Crosse County Sheriff's Department, was called out in 2009 on 233 calls in which he successfully completed eight tracks (for suspects), 182 drug searches, searched 271 cars, and had 102 "hits" or alerts to the presence of drugs. Of those alerts, 93 instances of drugs were found leading to 84 arrests. Cliff had an impressive reliability percentage of 91, when the legally acceptable percentage for K9s is only 54.

Boxers serve in SAR throughout the country; however, following 9/11, "Louie," a Boxer handled by his owner, Michele Verral, was the only Boxer deployed to work as a human remains scent detection dog at the Fresh Kills Landfill in Staten Island, New York. As tons upon tons of mangled building debris were brought for sifting at the landfill, this particular Boxer's job was to detect even the most remote, minute remains. Louie made 14 hits within 20 minutes, and continued working at this pace for days. With DNA testing, the remains were identified and then returned to their families. Louie's job did not mend hearts or absolve families of their pain; however, the Boxer's valuable work provided surviving family members with much-needed closure.

Boxers also are frequently trained to work as service dogs, such as seeing-eye dogs, hearing dogs, or assistance dogs. Many Boxer owners are involved with their dogs in volunteer pet visitation or animal-assisted therapy work, and thus spread "Boxer love" to an even greater audience.

Without a doubt, the Boxer continues to amaze his owners and handlers with the great breadth of work and service he can provide to humans. Perhaps the only limit to this breed is not with the dog itself, but in the caliber of his handler. In the right hands and with the proper instruction, the Boxer can and still does perform in a great variety of fields. And, as always, he understands how to "turn it on" and "turn it off," so even the working Boxer remains a beloved pet at home.

Introduction to America

The first Boxer to achieve a championship from the American Kennel Club (AKC) was rightfully a Boxer from Frau Stockmann's vom Dom kennels. A German champion or "Sieger," Dampf v Dom, owned by the governor of New York and his wife, finished his American championship in 1915. A few fanciers of the breed began forming in the Midwest during the 1920s, but it was not until the early 1930s that the breed really began its sweep across the country.

German Siegers were being imported and campaigned at shows, creating quite a stir among dog fanciers. As more people became familiar with the breed—and as more Boxers were awarded Best in Shows (BIS)—the popularity of the breed also continued to grow. In 1934 a powerful fawn male, International Champion Sigurd v Dom, was imported from Frau Stockmann's kennel, and began to set a few records of his own here. Along with two BIS, 43 Group Firsts, and 54 Best of Breed (BOB)—including one at Westminster Kennel Club's dog show in 1935—Sigurd also was recognized as a leading sire in the United States for many years.

In May 1935, the American Boxer Club (ABC) was approved by the AKC as a parent club for the Boxer. At the time, the ABC consisted of just 17 members. The Boxer was initially lumped into the Non-sporting group, but after petitioning the AKC, the Boxer was moved to the Working group where the breed belonged.

An item of great controversy among this small but growing breed club was the breed standard. Apparently, either a pre-1920 version of the German standard was translated into English and published, or an older Austrian standard was used. Therefore, the first standard that was adopted by the ABC was *not* the current German standard. The result was that the dogs that were being imported from Germany into the United States, as well as those that were being bred, did not conform to the standard. In 1938 the breed standard was revised, with the help of Philip Stockmann, who came to New York City to judge Boxers at Westminster in February, to more closely match the current German standard. The ABC now had more than 100 members. The largest Boxer kennel at the time was Mazelaine, owned by John Wagner. This kennel sometimes had anywhere from 80 to 100 Boxers.

The rest, as we say, is history. Even as U.S. involvement in World War II loomed, Boxer fever had already grabbed dog fanciers across the country and eventually would spread around the world. Many notable kennels would shine in the show ring and rack up honors and

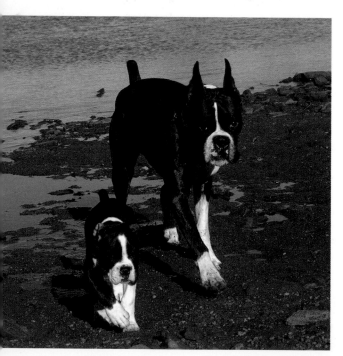

awards; to attempt to mention them here would require another book unto itself. However, any book on the Boxer would be remiss not to include one particular dog who is considered by many to be the changing force in American Boxer history: Ch. Bang Away of Sirrah Crest.

Bang Away of Sirrah Crest

In 1939 a doctor and his wife decided they wanted to become serious about breeding Boxers and founded a kennel in California called Sirrah Crest. Little did anyone know at the time that Dr. R. C. Harris and his wife, Phoebe, would breed the most winning Boxer of the century. ("Sirrah" is "Harris" spelled backward.) Purchasing two puppies from Wagner's Mazelaine kennel, the Harrises began their breeding program. In 1949 Bang Away of Sirrah Crest was born. Later that year, Frau Stockmann would visit the United States and would select the flashy fawn and white two-and-a-half-month old Boxer as Best in Match at a local puppy match. Stockmann pronounced that Bang Away would become America's greatest Boxer—and he did. In six years Bang Away had 121 Best in Show wins, including the coveted Westminster win.

Bang Away is credited with more than just a phenomenal number of wins and in bringing the popularity of Boxers to the top for more than a decade. Bang Away also brought striking style and a certain grace to the breed that is reflected even today in the nation's top Boxers.

Chapter Two
The Boxer Today

The Boxer today is a beautiful animal. He is both powerful and graceful, as well as penetratingly intelligent and whimsical. Though his roots remain in Germany, the Boxer has developed in the United States into his own outstanding version of a universally popular breed. He continues to be a ringside favorite at dog shows, and is adored by breed fanciers and the general dog-loving population alike.

Breed Standard

The following breed standard was revised by the American Boxer Club (ABC) in 2005. The standard is a description of the perfect Boxer. This Boxer, of course, has never existed, but breeders use the standard as a road map in developing their dogs. Occasionally the road map changes, too, as tastes in the United States change. For the most part, however, the standard is very similar to the first German standard upon which it is based.

General Appearance
The *ideal* Boxer is a medium-sized, square-built dog of good substance with short back, strong limbs, and a short, tight-fitting coat. His well-developed muscles are clean, hard, and appear smooth under taut skin. His movements denote energy. The gait is firm, yet elastic, the stride free and ground-covering, the carriage proud. Developed to serve as guard, working, and companion dog, he combines strength and agility with elegance and style. His expression is alert and his temperament steadfast and tractable.

The chiseled head imparts to the Boxer a unique individual stamp. It must be in correct proportion to the body. The broad, blunt muzzle is the distinctive feature, and great value is placed upon its being of proper form and balance with the skull.

In judging the Boxer, first consideration is given to general appearance and overall balance. Special attention is then devoted to the head, after which the individual body components are examined for their correct construction, and the gait evaluated for efficiency.

Size
Adult males 23 to 25 inches; females 21½ to 23½ inches at the withers. Proper balance and quality

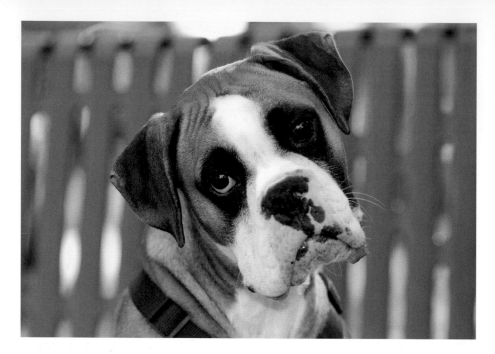

in the individual should be of primary importance since there is no size disqualification.

Proportion

The body in profile is square in that a horizontal line from the front of the forechest to the rear projection of the upper thigh should equal the length of a vertical line dropped from the top of the withers to the ground.

Substance

Sturdy with balanced musculature. Males larger boned than females.

Head

The beauty of the head depends upon the harmonious proportion of muzzle to skull. The blunt muzzle is ⅓ the length of the head from the occiput to the tip of the nose, and ⅔

the width of the skull. The head should be clean, not showing deep wrinkles (wet). Wrinkles typically appear upon the forehead when ears are erect, and are always present from the lower edge of the stop running downward on both sides of the muzzle.

Expression

Intelligent and alert.

Eyes

Dark brown in color, frontally placed, generous, not too small, too protruding, or too deep-set. Their mood-mirroring character, combined with the wrinkling of the forehead, gives the Boxer head its unique quality of expressiveness. Third eyelids preferably have pigmented rims.

Ears

Set at the highest point of the sides of the skull, the ears are customarily cropped, cut rather long and tapering, and raised when alert. If uncropped, the ears should be of moderate size, thin, lying flat and close to the cheeks in repose, but falling forward with a definite crease when alert.

Skull

The top of the skull is slightly arched, not rounded, flat, nor noticeably broad, with the occiput not overly pronounced. The forehead shows a slight indentation between the eyes and forms a distinct stop with the topline of the muzzle. The cheeks should be relatively flat and not bulge (cheekiness), maintaining the clean lines of the skull and should taper into the muzzle in a slight, graceful curve.

Muzzle and Nose

The muzzle, proportionately developed in length, width, and depth, has a shape influenced first through the formation of both jawbones, second through the placement of the teeth, and third through the texture of the lips. The top of the muzzle should not slant down (downfaced), nor should it be concave (dishfaced); however, the tip of the nose should lie slightly higher than the root of the muzzle. The nose should be broad and black.

Bite and Jaw Structure

The Boxer bite is undershot, the lower jaw protruding beyond the upper and curving slightly upward. The incisor teeth of the lower jaw are in a straight line, with the canines preferably up front in the same line to give the jaw the greatest possible width. The upper line of incisors is slightly convex with the corner upper incisors fitting snugly back of the lower canine teeth on each side. Neither teeth nor the tongue should ever show when the mouth is closed.

The upper jaw is broad where attached to the skull and maintains this breadth except for a very slight tapering to the front. The lips, which complete the formation of the muzzle, should meet evenly in front. The upper lip is thick and padded, filling out the frontal space created by the projection of the lower jaw, and laterally is supported by the canines of the lower jaw. Therefore, these canines must stand far apart and be of good length so that the front surface of the muzzle is broad and squarish and, when viewed from the side, shows moderate layback. The chin should be perceptible from the side as well as from the front. Any suggestion of an overlap obscuring the chin should be penalized.

Neck

Round, of ample length, muscular and clean without excessive hanging skin (dewlap). The neck has a distinctly arched and elegant nape blending smoothly into the withers.

Back and Topline

The back is short, straight, muscular, firm, and smooth. The topline is slightly sloping when the Boxer is at attention, leveling out when in motion.

Body

The chest is of fair width, and the forechest well defined and visible from the side. The brisket is deep, reaching down to the elbows; the depth of the body at the lowest point of the brisket equals half the height of the dog at the withers. The ribs, extending far to the rear, are well arched but not barrel shaped. .

The loins are short and muscular. The lower stomach line is slightly tucked up, blending into a graceful curve to the rear. The croup is slightly sloped, flat, and broad. The pelvis is long and in females especially broad. Tail is set high, docked, and carried upward. An undocked tail should be severely penalized.

Forequarters

The shoulders are long and sloping, close-lying, and not excessively covered with muscle (loaded). The upper arm is long, approaching a right angle to the shoulder blade. The elbows should not press too closely to the chest wall nor stand off visibly from it. The forelegs are long, straight, and firmly muscled and, when viewed from the front, stand parallel to each other. The pastern is strong and distinct, slightly slanting, but standing almost perpendicular to the ground. The dewclaws may be removed. Feet should be compact, turning neither in nor out, with well-arched toes.

Hindquarters

The hindquarters are strongly muscled with angulation in balance with that of the forequarters. The thighs are broad and curved, the breech musculature hard and strongly developed. Upper and lower thigh long. The legs are well angulated at the stifle, neither too steep nor overangulated, with clearly defined, well "let down" hock joints. Viewed from behind, the hind legs should be straight with hock joints leaning neither in nor out. From the side, the leg below the hock (metatarsus) should be almost perpendicular to the ground, with a slight slope to the rear permissible. The metatarsus should be short, clean, and strong. The Boxer has no rear dewclaws.

Coat

Short, shiny, lying smooth and tight to the body.

Color

The colors are fawn and brindle. Fawn shades vary from light tan to mahogany. The brindle ranges from sparse, but clearly defined black stripes on a fawn background, to such a heavy concentration of black striping that the essential fawn background color barely, although clearly, shows through (which may create the appearance of reverse brindling). White markings should be of such distribution as to enhance the dog's appearance, but may not exceed one-third of the entire coat. They are not desirable on the flanks

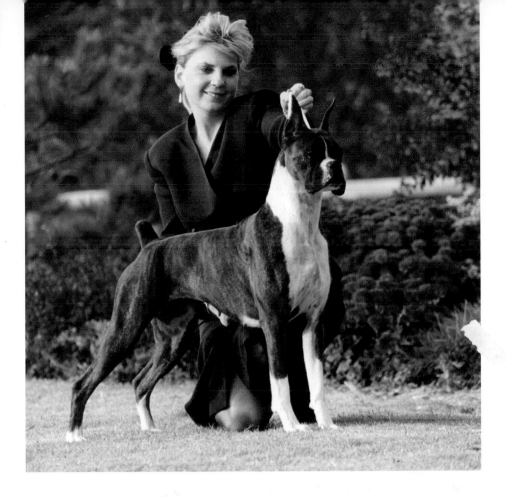

or on the back of the torso proper. On the face, white may replace part of the otherwise essential black mask and may extend in an upward path between the eyes, but it must not be excessive, so as to detract from true Boxer expression. The absence of white markings, the so-called "plain" fawn or brindle, is perfectly acceptable, and should not be penalized in any consideration of color. *Disqualifications*— Boxers that are any color other than

fawn or brindle. Boxers with a total of white markings exceeding one-third of the entire coat.

Gait

Viewed from the side, proper front and rear angulation is manifested in a smoothly efficient, level-backed, ground-covering stride with a powerful drive emanating from a freely operating rear. Although the front legs do not contribute impelling power, adequate reach should be evident to prevent interference, overlap, or sidewinding (crabbing). Viewed from the front, the shoulders should remain trim and the elbows not flare out. The legs are parallel until gaiting narrows the track in proportion to increasing speed, then the legs come in under the body but should never cross. The line from the shoulder down through the leg should remain straight, although not necessarily perpendicular to the ground. Viewed from the rear, a Boxer's rump should not roll. The hind feet should dig in and track relatively true with the front. Again, as speed increases, the normally broad rear track will become narrower. The Boxer's gait should always appear smooth and powerful, never stilted or inefficient.

Character and Temperament

These are of paramount importance in the Boxer. Instinctively a hearing guard dog, his bearing is alert, dignified, and self-assured. In the show ring, his behavior should exhibit constrained animation. With family and friends, his temperament is fundamentally playful, yet patient and stoical with children. Deliberate and wary with strangers, he will exhibit curiosity but, most importantly, fearless courage if threatened. However, he responds promptly to friendly overtures honestly rendered. His intelligence, loyal affection, and tractability to discipline make him a highly desirable companion. Any evidence of shyness, or lack of dignity or alertness, should be severely penalized.

The foregoing description is that of the ideal Boxer. Any deviations from the above-described dog must be penalized to the extent of the deviation.

Disqualifications

Boxers that are any color other than fawn or brindle. Boxers with a total of white markings exceeding one-third of the entire coat.

Approved February 11, 2005
Effective March 30, 2005
Reprinted courtesy of the American Boxer Club.

The Boxer in Other Countries

As mentioned earlier, over the last century the Boxer has evolved into an extremely popular dog in the United States. In England the Boxer is very similar, but it too has developed into a slightly different animal. Australian and Japanese Boxers also have a bit of uniqueness to them. There's no question that regardless of the country of origin, a Boxer is a Boxer; however, it is interesting to see how members of different countries and cultures view the "perfect" Boxer.

Perhaps the most striking difference in conformation in the Boxer is seen in the original home of the breed itself, Germany. Here, a strong emphasis on breeding working dogs has influenced the development of the breed, which is larger-boned, more heavily muscled, broader in head, and shorter in muzzle than its North American counterparts. The German Boxer's consistently outstanding performance in tracking, obedience, and protection work is also noticeable. (In Germany, Boxers are still actively used in police and military work.) German breeders also relate an extremely low incidence of white Boxers, and relatively few health problems.

But breeders are quick to point out that the German Boxer wasn't always this way, and that heart disorders and hip dysplasia plagued the breed in the 1960s. The introduction of the *Zuchttauglichkeitsprü-*

fung (ZTP or breeding qualification test) enabled the Boxer Klub of Germany to maintain minimum breeding requirements. The ZTP is credited with wiping out much of the German Boxer's health, temperament, and conformation problems.

ZTP

The ZTP was introduced in Germany in the late 1940s as an optional test to substantiate a Boxer's suitability for breeding. The test, which examines the Boxer's conformation, health, temperament, and working abilities, became a mandatory test for all Boxers seeking approval for breeding in 1974. Boxers who pass

the rigorous ZTP have their test results recorded and are then allowed to be bred. Any Boxer that does *not* pass the ZTP (only two chances are given) is proclaimed *Zuchtverbot* and cannot be bred—ever. If it is, the puppies are not allowed to be registered. In the United States, this would be similar to denying a Boxer the ability to register as a purebred; he would be "paperless."

The ZTP is constructed of three separate tests in which the Boxer must be graded: health, conformation, and temperament.

Health

In the health section of the test, the Boxer must be X-rayed for hip dysplasia and receive certification that he is free of it.

Note: Boxers with ratings of "transition" or "slight" are able to test for the ZTP; however, if they pass, these dogs must be bred to a Boxer that is certified clear of the disease. Next, the Boxer is tested for endurance through a 12.4-mile (20-km) trot alongside a bicycle, which is traveling roughly 7½ to 9 miles an hour (12 to 15 km/hour). The endurance test is used to prove the stamina of the Boxer—vital to a working dog—and to weed out "bad" hearts. Since the prevalent heart disorder in Germany is aortic stenosis (AS) rather than Arrhythmogenic Right Ventricular Cardiomyopathy (ARVC), Boxers with AS would likely have difficulties with this portion of the test (for more on these heart diseases, see Chapter Eleven).

The endurance test, however, is not considered sufficient by some members in dealing with heart problems. They want more. Currently, the Boxer Klub is encouraging owners to test their dogs for AS and other heart diseases. The test results are then recorded permanently on the dog's records and on any future pedigrees.

Another health test that is being promoted by the Boxer Klub is the spinal X-ray to detect spondylosis, a degenerative disease of the spine. The Boxer Klub currently maintains a list of Boxers who have had a spinal X-ray for spondylosis, as well as the dogs' results. This list is kept up to date and available for public viewing online at the breed club's website.

Conformation

Once the Boxer has passed all necessary health tests, he must now be presented to a judge to be graded in 63 different categories of conformation. Literally every aspect of the dog, from his eye color and tooth formation to his paws, is graded on a scale of one to five, with the number three position being the most favorable. Few Boxers fail the conformation exam because, as one longtime breeder noted, owners know if their dogs can pass or not, and if they can't, the owner doesn't attempt the ZTP.

Temperament

The final phase of the ZTP is the temperament test in which the Boxer is tested on his steadiness, protection abilities, and courage in a sort of "mini" *Schutzhund* test. For German Boxer owners, it is important for the heritage of the breed that Boxers retain their original temperament and prove they are good *Schutzdienst* (Schutzhund test takers).

1. In the steadiness portion of the test, the Boxer must walk on a relaxed leash alongside his owner and remain steady when, with no warning, a person fires off a gun at close range. The dog may not show fearfulness or aggressiveness.

2. In the protection portion of the temperament test, the Boxer is taken across a field—more than 50 yards (46 m)—by a person other than the dog's owner. The dog then watches as a person pretends to leap out and suddenly attack the dog's owner. The Boxer is released and, with no commands, must run down the attacker, bite the specially padded arm, and hold the bite until the owner gives the command "aus!" (out). The dog must then sit with no further biting or barking.

3. In the final section of the ZTP, the Boxer's courage is tested. The helper, a specially trained person who is heavily padded, runs straight for the Boxer and his owner, shouting in a loud, erratic, and menacing manner. On command, the Boxer must run to the attacker and bite the helper's arm. The dog must hold the arm—it's padded—until the owner can run to the dog and give him the *out* command and put him into a controlled *sit*.

Higher Titles and Red Papers

If this sounds like a lot of work to go through to be able to breed a dog, it is—but, to achieve an even higher status as a Boxer, the dog must go through additional tests. To achieve the advanced level of *Körung*, the Boxer must attain a Schutzhund title (Schutzhund involves obedience, tracking, and protection work), and must receive two "very good" ratings at two different dog shows. In Germany, all dogs are judged against the standard in the show ring and receive a rating *at each show,* along with a

copy of the judge's comments for that particular dog. Owning a Köered Boxer is important for two reasons. First, it allows the Boxer to be bred to *any* Boxer who has passed its ZTP. Second, the Boxer can now be selected to win special "winner" or "Sieger" titles at shows.

Restrictions in America?

Though interest groups have from time to time attempted to convince breeders that minimum health standards should be set in order for dogs to be bred in the United States, it is unlikely that American Boxer breeders would submit to the extensive restrictions presented by Germany's breeding requirements. However, there have been inroads made toward providing puppy buyers with similar information.

If a breeder permanently identifies his or her Boxers through microchipping or tattooing, the American Kennel Club will record the results of certain health tests and screenings with the dog's records. Conformation championships have always been recorded with the dog's information, as are performance event titles awarded in AKC events. All these records help to give the puppy buyer an indication of the background of the puppy, but the burden of finding out if a puppy comes from healthy stock with excellent conformation still weighs on the buyer.

Controversial Issues Facing the Breed

Every breed has its issues. How a breed club handles these issues, however, can greatly affect how the breed develops in the future. For the Boxer, there are three issues that are currently of interest to many fanciers: the white Boxer, cropped ears, and docked tails.

The White Boxer

In the early days of the breed, the Boxer came in many colors, including a large percentage of white and particolor or check dogs. Until World War I, the colors of white and parti-color were accepted by the German Boxer Klub. It is thought that during the war, however, the acceptance of this color fell out of favor when it was discovered that a white messenger dog was much more visible at night than a darkly colored dog. In 1925 white Boxers were ousted from the stud books, allowed back in temporarily in the 1930s, and then never accepted as an allowable color in that country again.

In the United States, the standard has always read that a dog with too much white possesses a disqualifying fault. Unfortunately, many years ago the American Boxer Club took a rather harsh stand on what to do with puppies that had this disqualifying fault. Club members were not allowed to sell, place, or breed a white Boxer. This left breeders faced with the decision either of keeping all the white puppies from every litter they bred, or euthanizing them. Neither choice was acceptable to many breeders, particularly when as much as 25 percent of every litter is white.

In the late 1990s the winds began to change. The ABC revised its restrictions to allow owners to place their white puppies, but maintained that the puppies could not be sold, registered, or bred. For many breeders, this was just the relaxation in the rule they were looking for.

Others, however, are looking for more. There are fanciers of white Boxers who would like to see the white Boxer accepted as an allowable color in the breed standard. They would also like to see the white Boxer used in breeding programs. This would be difficult, warn critics of the movement, because the white coat color is linked to genetic deafness, which would add one more health issue for breeders to worry about. Other breeders note that though they abide by the ABC's rule on white Boxers, they're not sure that summarily eliminating white Boxers from breeding programs isn't eliminating some of the best dogs.

Currently, white Boxer owners can get Purebred Alternative Listing (PAL) (see page 63 for an explanation of PAL) numbers for their dogs and compete in many of the AKC's performance events. Though the white Boxer is not in the show ring, it has made a permanent spot for itself in the hearts and homes of Boxer owners across the country.

Cropped Ears

To achieve the permanently erect ear of the Boxer, the ear must be trimmed to a point and the edges stitched to close the wound. The ears must then be taped and put in a rack so that they heal in the proper position and don't flop. The procedure is performed by a veterinarian with the Boxer under an anesthetic.

The breed's ears have been cropped in this fashion since the beginning of the breed. Since the late 1980s, however, it has been illegal in many countries to crop a dog's ears. (German Boxers have been sporting natural ears for nearly 20 years.)

In the United States, an increasing number of pet owners are not cropping their dogs' ears, either because they favor the look of the natural ear, or they simply don't want to spend the money and time necessary to insure that the cropped ears will heal correctly.

In the show ring, it was virtually unheard of to present a Boxer without cropped ears, but there are now many champions who are being finished with natural ears. This is largely due to a modification in the Boxer breed standard regarding ears. In the 1999 version, the standard only described the ideal Boxer ears as being cropped in a long, tapered fashion. Though uncropped ears were not listed as a disqualification, this natural ear type was also not described in the standard.

The breed standard was revised in 2005, to include guidelines for judging natural or uncropped ears. This revision effectively allowed Boxers with uncropped ears to be competitive in the show ring with cropped-ear Boxers.

Docked Tails

It seems that changes always affect the Boxers overseas first, and the repercussions of these changes then gradually ripple across the Atlantic to the United States. The latest controversy to hit Europe—and one that Boxer owners in this country are keeping an eye on—is that of the undocked tail. Boxer tails are generally docked by a veterinarian within the first few days following the puppies' birth. This is not so anymore in many European countries where tail docking has been banned and the Boxer has a full tail.

Most Boxers in the United States sport docked tails, and in the 2005 revision of the Boxer breed standard, wording was added to

the standard that details: "An undocked tail should be severely penalized." So a natural tail is not desirable in the show ring, but it is not a disqualification. This allows European Boxers (with natural ears and tails) to compete with American Boxers in the ring.

As for the Boxer as a pet or canine sports competitor, a full tail is fine. In fact, several German trainers relate that after decades of working with docked tails and now working with full tails, they believe the full tail gives the Boxer more balance and agility.

Yes, a Boxer wagging a full tail does look a bit different. It doesn't look bad, mind you, just very different. This is a tail with one muscular whip to it—and given the Boxer's joyful temperament, the greatest concern of owners may be in their own personal safety.

Chapter Three

The Boxer as a Companion

There are many reasons why the Boxer has been a consistent favorite with Americans and Canadians:

• The Boxer is a versatile breed that can adapt to many different living environments.

• He can and does do well at most anything.

• He excels at performance events just as much as he excels at being a favorite house pet.

• He will entertain and love a family of five, or be quite content as an "only child" of someone who is single.

• Finally, the Boxer is a strikingly handsome animal. It is virtually impossible to walk a well-cared-for Boxer without turning heads and being stopped by admiring dog lovers.

But the Boxer is not without his faults—or "challenges," as breed lovers would prefer to call them. So, before you make the decision to purchase a Boxer as your canine companion, it is important to balance the breed's strengths with its potential foibles. For many Boxer owners, the challenges of owning and caring for the breed that are listed in this chapter are considered minor and are readily accepted as part of the whole package. For other dog owners, however, what might be considered no big deal to a Boxer lover could be considered unbearable to someone who has not previously owned the breed.

Boxer Strengths

As mentioned above, the Boxer is a good-looking dog. A well-fed, conditioned Boxer has a glossy coat, well-defined muscles, and alert, penetrating eyes. The Boxer is attractive and varied in coloring as well, coming in a wide range of fawns and brindles, often with flashy white markings on the chest, neck, legs, and head—no two Boxers look alike. The short coat of the Boxer requires minimal care to keep it looking sleek.

Love of Family

Of course, the strengths of the Boxer go much deeper than his good-hearted bowling-over on occasion from an exuberant dog. Very small children should be supervised, simply because the dog's size and strength could accidently cause a small child to have a rather hard tumble.

The temperament of the Boxer is one that has not been diluted with his popularity. He remains a very loyal, even-tempered, gentle breed that often maintains his good sense even when treated very poorly. In dogs who are raised in nurturing environments, the number of ill-tempered Boxers is thought to be even less. This is not to say, of course, that there aren't Boxers in this world with poor temperaments. There are, but for a breed that has been popular for so many years, it's really quite amazing that there aren't more Boxers with poor temperaments.

Trainability

The Boxer is a very intelligent dog that is quite trainable. He thoroughly enjoys any and all opportunities to be with his master, and that includes daily training sessions. The versatility and athleticism of the breed also make him a good choice for a variety of competitive sports. Boxers are natural obedience dogs, and also perform well in agility, flyball, disk competitions, and Schutzhund.

Compatibility with Other Pets

And finally, the Boxer usually does well as a second pet with other

appearance. The Boxer is a very loyal, family-oriented dog. He is a natural watchdog to members of his family, and will bark quite furiously when a stranger comes to the door, but he is not normally an aggressive dog toward people. Once the visitor is invited into the home, a Boxer will revert from barking to furiously wagging his little docked tail.

Boxers enjoy being involved in everyday family life and, as a whole, love their families dearly. They make excellent pets for older children, or those children who don't mind a

Boxers, and other breeds of dogs. If an owner is considering owning more than one Boxer, or any dog for that matter, male-female pairings seem to fare the best overall. Male Boxers, particularly if neutered, can live peacefully (and playfully) with other males, and females have been known to get along fine with other females. However, if a Boxer decides he doesn't like a particular Boxer in the home, he may hold a lifelong grudge. In instances such as these, permanent separation will be necessary to prevent either dog from seriously injuring the other.

Boxers also can fare well with other pet species, such as cats and "pocket" pets (hamsters, gerbils, mice), if the Boxer is raised with these other pets as a puppy.

Boxer Challenges

The Boxer is a wonderful dog, but no breed of dog is perfect; Boxers have their imperfections, too. Often, new Boxer owners quickly find that the challenges of owning a Boxer fall into one of three categories:

1. cute, endearing, and forgivable.
2. slightly annoying but workable.
3. totally incompatible.

How you categorize the challenges of owning a Boxer is an individual decision; however, before buying a Boxer, you should give serious consideration to the breed's less desirable traits, and decide how well you will handle these breed characteristics. Keep in mind, too, that most dog ownership "problems" are solvable if the owner is patient, creative, and willing to make the necessary lifestyle changes to comfortably accommodate his or her canine companion. Following are important points to consider in owning a Boxer.

Training is a must. The Boxer is neither a particularly tall nor heavy dog, but he is extremely strong. Without any conditioning whatsoever, a five-month-old puppy is capable of taking his owner for a not-so-merry romp around the block. A gleeful greeting at the front door from an

unruly adolescent could also easily topple an adult who is less steady on his or her feet. For these reasons, immediate and consistent training is a must. Puppies should be enrolled in puppy kindergarten as soon as their veterinarians give the OK. Most veterinarians like to make sure that young puppies have received enough vaccinations to be immune to a variety of common deadly diseases. Adult dogs who are being adopted should also be enrolled in a training class, and the owner should work with the dog daily until it has reached a sufficient level of obedience.

Basic obedience training is the best investment you can make in your Boxer. Sure, it's time-consuming and it does cost money, but once you become involved with your Boxer's training, chances are you'll discover it's a lot of fun. In the long run, training your dog for 10 months to a year will help you achieve a well-behaved, welcome member of the family. If your puppy or dog is cherished, owning it will be a pleasure, not a pain.

The Boxer's activity level can be high. If you are used to a dog that gently wags his tail when you come in the door at night and then takes up his resident spot in front of the hearth, you might find the activity level of the Boxer a little more than you're accustomed to experiencing.

Boxers do move around a bit. On a scale of 1 to 10, with "1" being dead and "10" being perpetual, non-stop motion—they're either moving or they're sleeping and they're hardly ever sleeping—the Boxer would range in the 5 to 6 zone. Basically, if the Boxer gets sufficient exercise throughout the day, he won't drive you crazy. What's a sufficient amount of exercise? A good morning romp, a midday walk, and another evening romp will do just fine. Or, if you don't have a yard in which your dog can really stretch his legs, three, 20-minute vigorous walks should take care of most young and middle-aged dogs.

Regular exercise will take the energetic edge off your dog, but don't expect your Boxer to resign himself to a quiet corner in the room. Once inside, the Boxer will continue to gently—and sometimes not so gently—demand attention. You may find your Boxer following you from room to room and sitting close to you for you to stroke him. Or your Boxer may drop toy after toy at your feet until he can entice you into a game of tug-of-war or indoor catch. Some dog owners find this canine attention annoying; others see it as one of the behaviors that is endearing in the Boxer. How you evaluate this activity level is entirely up to your expectations of what a dog should or shouldn't be. So, if you prefer a dog that is less demonstrative in its affections, a Boxer may not be for you.

Boxers cannot tolerate excessive heat or cold. The Boxer is not an outdoor dog and does not do well in extremely cold or hot weather. Its short, sleek coat will not keep the dog warm for any extended periods of time in the winter.

If the temperature is too high, your Boxer will suffer, too. As a brachycephalic (short-nosed) breed, the Boxer is less efficient at cooling himself off than other, longer-nosed breeds. He can't tolerate very hot days even if he has a shady place to rest outside. The Boxer also can't be expected to compete in any taxing performance events, such as flyball or agility, on a hot summer day.

Boxers are destructive when bored or lonely. Boxers love their people and do not like to be separated from them for any period of time. If left alone, the Boxer will think of ways to amuse himself, or he will

try to rejoin his family. In the backyard, a bored Boxer might choose to dig a trench in your prized rose bed, remove and destroy a newly planted sapling, or simply chew through a wood post in your deck. Inside, the neglected Boxer may decide your windows look better without blinds, or that two carpets, in asymmetrical sections, fit the room better than one. If the Boxer is outside and wants to come inside to be with you, you could find a screen door off its hinges.

Yes, Boxers have been known to do all of these things and more. A happy Boxer, however, does not do these things. Why? Two reasons. A happy Boxer gets to live with his family. His activities are supervised and, because he receives lots of interaction and love from humans, the happy Boxer is less likely to become lonely, bored, and destructive. When the Boxer cannot be supervised—for example, if the owner is going out to dinner for a few hours—the wise owner makes sure the Boxer is exercised, watered, properly relieved, and then put into his crate with a good chew toy.

Agility takes a toll. The Boxer is very agile and nimble. These admirable qualities, however, can be troublesome if used at the wrong place at the wrong time. For example, the counter-jumping ability of the Boxer can be frustrating when you have company coming in less than five minutes and your Boxer has plucked the cooling roast from your kitchen counter and taken it to the backyard to devour. The dog's agility, coupled with the breed's good sense of smell, makes a situation in which literally nothing is safe on the counters, tabletops, or other "in-reach" surfaces. So, if you're used to leaving bonbons on the coffee table or bread on the kitchen counter, you'll want to find new places for these foods or restrict your Boxer from these irresistible temptations.

Cleverness can be a drawback. Can a dog be too smart for his own good? Perhaps. If so, the Boxer may be a candidate for the canine Mensa club. Boxers can figure out how to open latches, pull open drawers, and even raid refrigerators. They can also be very determined in their cleverness. If at first a Boxer doesn't succeed at getting what he wants, he may try again and again and again—each time in a different

way—until he *does* succeed. Boxer owners are generally amused at their dogs' cleverness, but this trait also requires that the owners remain one step ahead of their dogs.

The drawbacks of being a bit too clever can also extend into a Boxer's obedience and performance event training. Since the Boxer learns so quickly, he must be kept interested in the task at hand if he is to continue to perform that task. In other words, if the dog's training is not kept lively and interesting, the Boxer often finds ways to "untrain" himself.

Sloppy dinner manners: The Boxer's mouth, teeth, and lips were not designed for black tie dining. Remember, this breed has a jaw that was meant to be able to bite and hold onto his prey or opponent. What this means is that today's Boxer, which retains the physical equipment to bite but is not a "biter" as such, is not a very neat eater. In fact, when a Boxer is eating, he is not a very pretty sight. Boxer owners are used to their dogs' sprinkling of dinner remnants around the food bowl, but owners of neater-eating breeds might be a bit shocked—and perhaps a bit distraught—by the amount of after-dinner floor cleaning that is necessary. Drinking water can also be a real event for the un-Boxerized owner. As with any longer-lipped breed, water is often held in the dog's upper hanging lips, and dribbled across the floor as the dog moves away from his bowl.

Drooling: The Boxer is not any worse at drooling than breeds of similar lip construction; however, if you are used to a tight-lipped breed that does not drool at all, and the idea of a dog occasionally drooling when he is excited, when he has just been exercising, or when he spots something he would really like to eat, then you might want to think about this.

Flatulence: Oh yes, and there's this little issue of bad gas. Boxers tend to produce copious amounts of fragrant fumes after they have consumed their meals. This can be quite offensive to owners of more delicate constitutions, but most Boxer owners take it in stride. The reason for the flatulence is believed to be connected to the breed's difficulties digesting certain foods. Much of a dog's after-dinner condition may be controlled through a carefully selected diet.

Health issues: The Boxer as a breed is susceptible to some diseases and conditions that could substantially shorten his lifespan (see Chapter Eleven: Common Diseases of the Boxer). Though many owners accept these risks as part of the Boxer package, and practice as much preventive veterinary care as possible, other dog owners simply don't want to add these worries to dog ownership. Prospective Boxer owners would be well advised to be as educated as possible about these diseases and conditions and make sure they select a puppy or adopt an adult who has the least possible chance of developing problems later in life.

Owners should look for puppies with parents and grandparents, if possible, who have been tested for serious hereditary diseases such as hip dysplasia, ARVC, and subaortic stenosis. Keep in mind, however, that even generations of documented, healthy, long-lived parentage is no absolute guarantee of perfect health, though it greatly enhances the dog's chances of living a healthy life.

Before You Buy

You've weighed the pros and cons of Boxer ownership and are willing to make the relationship work. Now, you must take a good, hard, and honest look at yourself, your loved ones, and your lifestyle to make sure you can and are able to make the changes necessary to create a healthy, nurturing environment for your new Boxer.

Meeting the Boxer

Before you have firmly decided to purchase or adopt a Boxer, take time to visit with Boxer breeders and owners.

• Observe how these Boxer lovers handle their dogs.

• Note how the breed interacts with humans—both familiar and strange. (Be prepared to be licked a *lot*.)

• If you are married and/or have children, watch how your family members interact with the adult dogs. Everyone loves a puppy, but how do your loved ones respond to a bouncy, playful, 60-lb. (27-kg) red brindle female with cropped ears

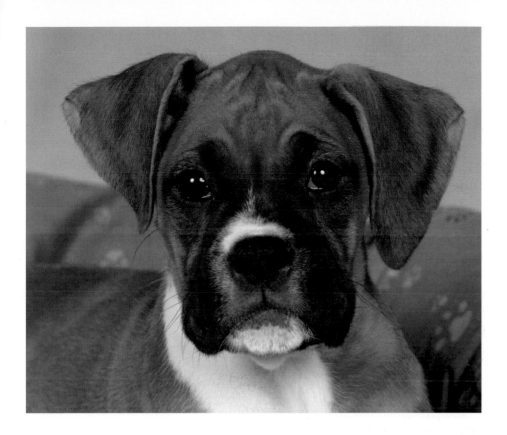

that looks kind of ferocious? Do your children quickly overcome the appearance of the dog and seem to enjoy being around the dog? Or do they run for cover?

• If you live in a household of more than one, it is very important for the success of the dog in the home that everyone in that household admires and enjoys the Boxer. There have been far too many rescue stories of households with mixed emotions over the dog. The Boxer usually loses in these instances and ends up being relinquished to the care of a rescue organization or turned into the local pound. Don't let this be your story!

Evaluating Your Available Time

Do you work long hours at your job? Do you have small children? Are you driving from activity to activity every night of the week? If your time is already thin, you will need to either rearrange your schedule and your priorities, or postpone adding a dog to your life at the present. Since daily training and exercise are required with Boxer ownership, you will need to carve out time for these activities. If time is tight and you still want a dog *now,* make sure you have a fat bank account, because you'll need a good supply of cash to make sure a dog walker can give your Boxer the daily exercise he needs, as well as a professional trainer to work with your dog on a daily basis.

Knowing Your Finances

As mentioned above, depending on your situation, dog ownership may be very expensive. On average, the first year of owning a dog can cost more than $2,000—and that's if everything goes well and you don't

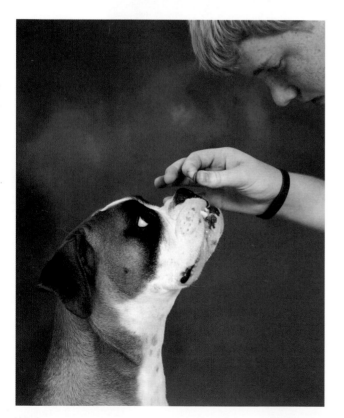

need any emergency surgeries to patch up torn skin or repair an injured foot. Subsequent years may cost less, but they may not. According to some estimates, an average, healthy midsize dog costs approximately $1,000 a year to maintain. If this is not in your budget, you may want to wait before purchasing a Boxer. This is not a breed that can flourish under poor conditions.

Considering Your Living Arrangements

Are you a homeowner, or do you rent? If you rent, be sure to check the renter's agreement to see whether you are allowed a pet, what the size limits are, and how much the monthly pet fee is *before* you purchase a Boxer. Rental properties frequently restrict renters to a 20-lb. (9-kg) dog limit. An adult Boxer does not meet this requirement! Also, many rental properties charge a hefty deposit prior to the arrival of a new pet, as well as a monthly fee as high as $50 a pet or more. You may also be required to provide proof of owning a good dog through letters from previous neighbors and your veterinarian. This can be troublesome if this is your first dog, because providing this type of proof is impossible.

Another consideration renters should concern themselves with is how often they move. Frequent moves are not impossible if the owner is committed to moving the Boxer as if he were a family member. In some instances, this may mean more extensive house hunting,

Can You Afford a Boxer?

Dogs are expensive, and Boxers are no exceptions. The following is a list of expenses you can expect to incur in your first year of owning a Boxer.

Crate (large)	$100
Pad for crate	$50
Pet gates (2)	$80
Pet stain and odor remover (1 gallon [3.8 l])	$20
Various chew toys	$30
"Anti-chewing" spray (16-oz. spray)	$7
"Big dog" scoop	$17
Dog food (quality)	$400
Dog bowls (ceramic or no-tip stainless steel) (2)	$20
Dental kit (toothbrush, toothpaste, finger brush)	$6
Adjustable collars (2)	$10
Matching 6-ft. (1.8-m) leash	$9
Personalized dog tag	$5
Toenail clippers, styptic powder	$17
Brush	$12
Dog shampoo, conditioner (concentrated; 1 gallon [3.8 l])	$35
Doses of flea and tick control (12)	$150
Heartworm preventive	$100
Routine veterinary care	$200
Obedience classes (10 months)	$200
First Year Total	**$1,468**

Other:	
Fencing for yard	$300–$1,000+
Dog door	$100–$250
Boarding, kennel (2-week vacation)	$170
Spay/Neuter	$120–$200+

or even special arrangements to have food shipped, as in temporary overseas moves.

Level of Commitment

Successful dog ownership really boils down to one simple element: the level of commitment of the owner. A committed owner is one who willingly will do whatever it takes to create an environment that is safe, healthy, and happy for his or her Boxer and does not try to skimp or cut corners in the care of the dog. A committed owner is well educated as to the needs and behaviors of the Boxer, and knows how to handle most situations, or is willing to seek advice from experienced Boxer owners. With a committed owner, there really isn't any dog ownership obstacle that can't be overcome by using a little creativity and a lot of determination.

Do You Have What It Takes?

The Boxer is a wonderful breed with many strengths and few weak-

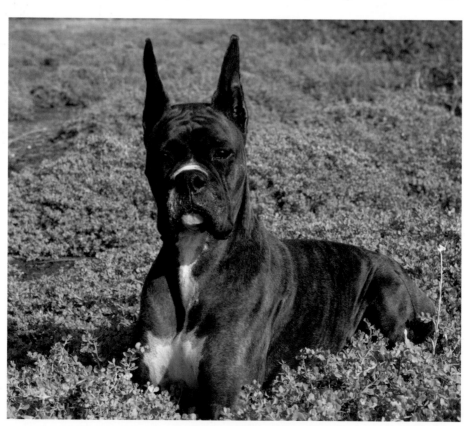

Children and Boxers

It is a common misconception that kids and dogs go together like peanut butter and jelly. They don't. Children must be taught how to interact appropriately with a puppy or dog, and the dog must be taught how to behave around children. Boxers are not known to have problems with aggression to people, though there are always rare exceptions, so a cautious parent should *never* entirely rule this out with any dog. Most often, however, injuries to children occur because the Boxer is a big, enthusiastic dog, and is easily capable of accidently toppling a small child. For this reason, parents of young children need to provide continuous, close-range supervision of all dog-child play, or be able to separate the child from the dog during unsupervised times. To do otherwise is inviting an accident to occur.

nesses, but, as previously discussed, it is not a perfect dog and It Is definitely not the dog for everyone. And, even if this *is* the dog for you, the timing may be all wrong. If all the pieces are not in place in your life for you to welcome a Boxer into your home, then hold off on your purchase. Make changes as necessary in your home first. Maybe you need to wait for your little ones to get a little older. Or, perhaps you need to work on scheduling less in your life and making more time for yourself,

your family, and later, a new dog. If finances are a sticking point, begin by stashing some cash in a savings account for the dog's care; just because *now* is not the right time, doesn't mean you can't begin planning for a Boxer in the future.

Of course, if the time is right, and this is the dog for you, you can begin your search for a new Boxer. Whether you decide to purchase a puppy or adopt an adult dog, if you choose carefully and raise your Boxer right, he will very quickly become a loyal and devoted family member.

Chapter Four

Choosing the Best Boxer for You

The Boxer Puppy

There may not be anything more adorable than a Boxer puppy. His floppy ears, dark eyes, and wrinkled, quizzical looks are enough to melt any dog owner's heart. The breed's flashy coloring in rich fawns and exotic brindles further enhances the attraction to this breed. Mix in the Boxer puppy's propensity to take part in high-energy play, and you have a recipe for a stunning, lovable puppy who is extremely entertaining just to watch. But don't expect to remain a casual observer when there's a Boxer puppy around. These puppies are always up for a good game, no matter what the game or who is playing—and you *will* play!

Quality

A reputable breeder will always register his or her litter; however, not *all* registered litters are from reputable breeders. An AKC registration is not a symbol of quality, but AKC show and performance titles—along with health tests—are.

In a word, Boxer puppies are irresistible. Quick to learn, eager to please, and a wriggly bundle of warmth and love, a Boxer puppy is a delight to be around—at least for a few minutes. Sure, puppies are cute; if they weren't, no human being could put up with the endless chores, home furnishings destruction, sleepless nights, and just plain hard work that is involved in raising a puppy in a healthy and loving environment. That's not to say that raising a puppy doesn't have its delightful moments and lasting rewards, but rearing a puppy into a well-mannered, delightful member of the family takes work and commitment. For many Boxer owners, the benefits of puppy ownership far outweigh the drawbacks. Dog lovers who aren't sure they're quite up to the intensive care of a little puppy, however, may find adopting an adult dog is a better option.

Adopted adult Boxers make wonderful pets and can be less challenging in many ways than a puppy (see Adopting the Adult Boxer, Chapter Five); there are many adults in need of homes. But if a puppy is what you really want, consider making a donation to Boxer Rescue to help those grown-up pups get a second chance on life.

Benefits and Drawbacks of Puppy Ownership

Most Boxer owners buy their dogs as puppies. Most of these puppies do well in their new homes, but some do not. The American Boxer Rescue Association (ABRA) reports that literally thousands of Boxers—from young puppies to aging adults—are given up to shelters and rescues across the country each year. Sadly, many of those owners relinquishing Boxers had purchased their puppies on a whim or based on emotions. Once the cuteness is gone, the Boxer is a goner.

Puppy love is a powerful force to which many dog lovers succumb. When the reality sinks in about how much work a puppy actually is, and what a lifestyle change this bundle of fur brings about, many new puppy owners' commitment wanes. Those owners who make a planned, educated decision to embark on raising a puppy, and who have a thorough understanding for what job lies ahead, usually do very well. Basically, raising a puppy requires the support of all family members, a good dose of commitment, a bit of creativeness to work out any poten-

tial problems, and a "do-whatever-it-takes" mind-set to make the human-dog relationship succeed.

So, before you launch into purchasing a puppy, it is critical you understand exactly what a Boxer puppy is really like. You also should be familiar with the level of care that is necessary to raise an energetic puppy, the time you will spend training the puppy in order to have a well-mannered adult, and the necessary financial commitment of raising a puppy; the first year can be expensive.

Good News About Puppy Ownership

Obviously, one of the greatest attractions of owning a puppy is that they are incredibly cute. They play a lot and will entertain their owners constantly with their silly and endearing antics—but there are more good reasons for purchasing a puppy besides simply being able to enjoy the dog's once-in-a-lifetime puppy stage.

One of the most important draws to buying a Boxer puppy is that the puppy is impressionable and moldable when he is young. You, as the owner, have the ability to take this eager puppy and give him the love and training he needs to develop into a wonderful family dog and devout companion. With the correct environment, you can strongly influence the dog's adult temperament and behaviors, and help him to become a social, well-mannered pet.

Another benefit to raising a puppy is that you can influence much of the Boxer's current and future health. By scheduling regular preventive veterinary care, conducting screenings for disease at appropriate ages, and providing a healthy, nutritious diet, an owner can help a Boxer to mature as disease-free as possible.

Also, if you want to compete with your Boxer, choosing a puppy may allow you to find a good potential prospect for your chosen sport, without paying large sums of money for a dog who is already proven in that area. For example, if you plan on showing your Boxer, you can much more affordably purchase a puppy with show potential than attempt to buy an adult dog with the same qualities. If you are looking for an obedience, agility, or *Schutzhund* prospect, the same is also true.

Raising a Boxer from a puppy also allows you to acclimate your dog to your lifestyle. If you have a family, rearing a puppy carefully with children and teaching him to respect little humans with unsteady gaits may be easier and safer than introducing an adult dog into the family who hasn't had experience with children and therefore is, perhaps, more cautious or fearful of children. If you have cats or other small non-canine pets, a puppy often is more accepting of living with a cat and may or may not realize the size difference when he (the Boxer) is fully grown.

Young puppies are fairly agreeable to settle into just about any lifestyle. Do you enjoy boating? A young Boxer will be more likely to enjoy swims and rides if he is acclimated to this water life early, though it is true that old dogs *can* learn new tricks. If you travel a lot, acclimating a puppy to regular road trips can be easier—and less of a cleanup—than with an adult dog.

Training can be easier, too, if you start with a young pup. With a lot of encouragement, a few yummy treats, and regular practice, a Boxer puppy often can learn the basic commands of sit, down, stay, and come by the time he is 16 weeks old. It's much easier to get a little, 12-lb. (5.4-kg) Boxer pup to sit with a treat than it is to teach a boisterous, 60-plus-lb. (27-plus-kg), untrained adult the same maneuver. Additionally, there are some activities, such as tracking and other scent work, that many trainers say are best if the puppy is introduced to the beginning stages when he is very young.

Pitfalls of Puppyhood

Puppyhood is not all fun and games, however, and there are some aspects of raising a puppy that involve a lot of time and work. In other words, it may be easier to train a Boxer when he is young and small, but you have to make the commitment to actually train the puppy. That means a one-hour class at least once a week for 10 months, and daily sessions working on what you've learned, ranging in time from five minutes several times a day for little puppies, to 20 minutes or more every day for older puppies. In addition to formal training, puppy owners must be committed to acclimating their new charges to the puppy's surroundings. This means socializing the puppy with other dogs, other people, and the things that happen in the neighborhood. If you, as a Boxer owner, don't resolve yourself to carve out this time for your Boxer's training, your young, strong Boxer very quickly will be out of control and will be less than desirable as a pet.

Note: Now may be a good time to mention that lack of training is

Temperament: Part Hereditary, Part Environment

One theory of temperament is that when a puppy is born, he will have inherited one of three possible temperaments: a steady, sound temperament, an "extreme" temperament (either aggressive or very fearful or shy), or a temperament that could develop into either a steady or an unstable one, depending on the environment the puppy is exposed to while growing up. It is also thought that the numbers of inherently "good" or "bad" puppies—those who no matter what you do will still have the temperament they were born with—is very small; therefore, the bulk of the puppies born can go either way.

So keep in mind when rearing your impressionable puppy that the environment you provide for him can make a drastic difference in the pup's behavior and temperament as he matures.

cited as the primary reason dogs are euthanized. In recent studies investigating why dogs were turned in to shelters, it was found that if a dog had little or no training, he had a very high chance of being turned in to the shelter. Conversely, if a dog had received training, he wasn't nearly as likely to be turned in to a shelter.

This makes sense: An untrained dog is no fun to live with. The problem many owners have is that they find puppy antics "cute" and see no reason to begin the puppy's training. The puppy quickly grows into an adolescent, a full-size dog with the activity level and mind-set of a puppy. This combination spells trouble and is trying for even the most patient and understanding owner. Though the dog is still trainable at this age, many overwhelmed owners simply banish the dog to the backyard, where he barks, digs, and climbs fences. When a family member ventures out to see the dog, the person is bowled over by a tremendously excited dog. It's usually not long after this stage that the dog makes a trip to the shelter.

Don't make this mistake with your Boxer puppy. Be sure to begin early with your pup's training and stick to it. At the year's end, you'll be the one with the well-trained dog and the envy of the neighborhood.

Play: Speaking of out of control, that's how most Boxer puppies play—at high speeds and without any care about what damage they might inflict on themselves or the things they crash into during their play. By nature, the Boxer is generally a breed with lots of energy. A well-trained adult Boxer can focus his energy on supervised play and, if given a job to perform, the adult is able to channel his energy into his work. Puppies, of course, have no job except to play, investigate, and generally look for trouble. They require constant supervision in addition to opportunities for energetic play.

Teething: All puppies go through the dreaded teething stage. At around 16 weeks to five months, the puppy's milk teeth fall out and the adult teeth begin moving in. This physical change causes a normally chewy Boxer puppy to become a voracious one. Table legs, siding, small trees, and other objects may become the target of a teething Boxer puppy. One look at a Boxer's teeth and the strength of its bite should be an indicator of the level of destruction these babies are capable of, given a free moment.

House-training: House-training is another issue that must be addressed with puppy ownership. No puppy is perfect, and some are not as good at alerting owners to their elimination needs as others. Politely put, there are going to be accidents. Crates are going to need hosing down and carpets will need scrubbing. It's part of puppyhood. The benefit, however, is that when a pup makes a "mistake," it is less of an accident to clean than when an adult dog eliminates inappropriately.

Change in lifestyle: Then there's the abrupt change in a carefree lifestyle that a puppy brings. If you're used to total freedom, dashing out to join friends for the evening, taking off for a weekend getaway, or even spending the day at the beach, this will all change when you own a puppy. Your puppy will need to be fed at least three times a day. He will need to be exercised. He will need regular walks to allow him to relieve himself. A puppy can't be left in the backyard to fend for himself; he must be supervised just as you would a young child. And don't expect to sleep much in the first few days and weeks after you bring your puppy home. Your puppy will not be happy being separated from his littermates and mother, nor will he be happy to be separated from you. You'll find it amazing (perhaps distressfully so) how loudly a 10-lb. (4.5-kg) puppy can yelp and howl all by himself.

Expense: Finally, as mentioned in the previous chapter, puppies can be expensive. With vaccinations,

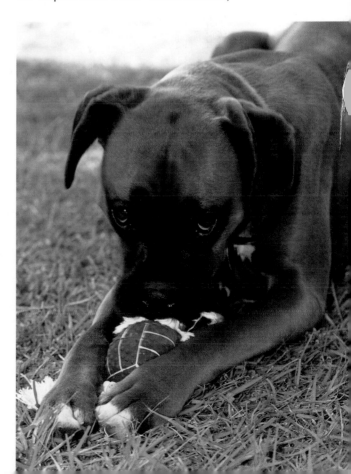

veterinary exams, ear cropping, and basic supplies, first-year expenditures can *easily* top $1,000.

So, is raising a Boxer puppy a challenge you can handle? If not, that's fine. Perhaps an adult Boxer would fit into your lifestyle better at this time. Or perhaps a Boxer just isn't realistically in the picture at all right now. That's all right, too. The important point to realize here is that if you go into puppy ownership with your eyes open and a commitment to make the relationship work no matter what happens, you will be successful.

Finding a Breeder You Can Trust

All breeders are not created equally—nor are their dogs. In general, you get what you pay for when buying a Boxer puppy. If you want a good family Boxer, you'll need to find a good breeder. If you want a great Boxer with show or performance event potential, you'll need to seek out and work with only the most reputable breeders who specialize in breeding Boxers for conformation or working/performance events. This is not to say that you can't find a nice pet from another puppy source, but it's much tougher and really not a job for someone who is new to the breed.

You might ask, "Why should I pay hundreds of dollars to a breeder for a Boxer that's just going to be a pet,

when I can pick one up from a newspaper ad for less than $100?" The simple reason is that the Boxer breed has enough potential health problems to justify searching for a dog that has been bred specifically to avoid or lessen the chances of having these illnesses. If you purchase a Boxer for a small sum from a breeder who doesn't X-ray his or her dogs for hip dysplasia, or test his or her dogs for ARVC, or worry about skin allergies, you may end up paying more for the puppy's health care in his first year of life than double or triple the purchase price of a healthier, well-bred puppy. So, how can you tell if a breeder is good, great, or "other"?

The Best of the Best

Of the thousands of Boxers that are bred each year, probably only several hundred litters are from breeders with impeccable standards. These are breeders who have been actively showing and competing with their Boxers for years and even decades. Boxers are a love, a passion, and an expensive hobby for these people. Breeding Boxers is not a money-making venture for them. Top breeders have litters only when they are trying to achieve another quality Boxer for themselves, not because they're trying to make a few bucks. In fact, when a breeder takes extreme care and planning with each litter, the puppies—though perhaps more expensive than a backyard product—are not sold at a profit. Most breeders of this caliber relate that when a litter is properly planned and cared for, the puppies are sold at a loss to the breeder.

When a quality, experienced breeder has a litter, he or she has bred for soundness of conformation and health, as well as for a solid, happy Boxer temperament. If you are searching for a pet, this quality breeding is still important. In addition to being a good-looking dog, a well-bred puppy should be very robust and healthy and should have that classic, loving Boxer temperament. Breeding for these qualities takes a lot of time, research, breed knowledge, and hard work.

Breeding for Looks

Experienced breeders know the breed standard inside out and upside down, and could probably recite it verbatim with their eyes closed. They know what is considered the perfect form for a Boxer. They also understand that there has never been a Boxer without one or more deviations from the standard or flaws in either how the dog is physically put together—slope of the shoulder, shape of the eye, position of the bite—or how he moves. However, these breeders continue their efforts to work a little closer toward that "perfect" dog.

How do they do this? They track their own bloodlines and have a solid understanding of what traits or characteristics are strong (dominant) in their lines and which are weak or recessive in their lines. These breeders also know how to breed to bring out the best in their dogs, and to suppress any weak points. When they plan a breeding, these breeders will spend a great deal of time researching and considering prospective mates for their dogs. Typically, the breeder searches for a suitable stud dog for a particular female. If the breeder has selected the correct mate, the stud's traits should counter or negate the female's faults, and vice versa. The goal of the resulting litter, therefore, should be an improvement over both parents.

Despite this careful planning, only a few pups in each litter may be recognizable, outstanding show quality. These puppies will have the potential to finish their conformation championships and, if they develop into particularly outstanding dogs, they may be able to be campaigned as "specials," competing for group and best in show wins. The remaining littermates will still be well-built, attractive Boxers. What this means to you as the pet owner is that you will have a great-looking dog with the form, function, and movement to participate in a wide variety of activities, both competitive and noncompetitive. The experienced breeder, as opposed to a novice or an inexperienced breeder, will be better able to determine which puppies may develop into show-quality and which will probably not. They will also be able to help an owner select a puppy whose temperament meshes well with the needs of the potential owner.

Breeding for Health

The breeder whose goal is breeding quality Boxers takes the extra step to certify the health of his or her dogs *before* breeding them. Quality breeders will test their dogs for ARVC and will *not* breed a dog who has been determined to have the disease through a genetic test. They will also be careful in breeding a dog who has been determined to be a carrier of the disease to a Boxer who has been tested free of the disease. Breeders will also test and certify that their Boxers are free of hip dysplasia. A certification number from the Orthopedic Foundation for Animals or PennHIP should appear on the mature Boxer's pedigree. The dogs should be certified for vision with the Canine Eye Registration Foundation (CERF) and many will have a DNA registration. The Boxers being bred should also be permanently identified, either through tattooing or microchipping (see Chapter Six). The American Kennel Club requires this permanent identification in order to record the individual health certificate registration numbers on the dog's permanent pedigree.

In addition to testing and certifying that the dogs being bred are free from inherited diseases, and thereby optimizing the probability that the ensuing puppies will be healthy, too, a good breeder also stands behind what he or she breeds.

Reputable breeders do this by offering all new puppy owners a written guarantee of their puppy's health. If the puppy has a serious health problem, the breeder will take the puppy back and will either refund the puppy owner's money or provide the person with another puppy. Also, if a puppy doesn't work out in a new owner's home *for any reason,* the reputable breeder will take that puppy back—and at any age.

Breeding for Temperament

Good breeders go beyond breeding for good looks and healthy dogs; they also breed for great temperaments. Dogs with questionable temperaments are simply not bred, even if the dog or bitch has his or her conformation championship. A poor temperament—aggression or severe shyness toward people—is considered a serious flaw and, given the size of the breed and the power of its bite, a quirky Boxer could inflict serious injuries. Though a bite on the ankle from a toy breed may be brushed aside and quickly forgiven, a chomp from a Boxer becomes a serious issue.

The Boxer, fortunately, is renowned for his affable, playful, even comical temperament. Though fierce-looking, this breed *rarely* displays any aggression toward people unless he has been seriously mistreated or poorly bred. With this in mind, the reputable breeder does not even consider breeding a Boxer unless he has the true Boxer temperament and is steady and trusting with people.

What this relates to is that instead of worrying if a puppy has the potential to be aggressive toward people or not, a puppy owner can focus his or her concerns on choosing the Boxer pup that has the best personality to fit his or her lifestyle. Experienced breeders know what temperaments work well with active individuals, what traits are good for families with small children, and what pups will fit into a more structured environment. You'll find that a quality breeder will be not only an excellent "dog person," but will also have the innate skills of a behaviorist and a psychiatrist, too.

The junkyard dog: Because the Boxer has a rather fierce look to those who don't know the marshmallow inside, there are people who will attempt to take him and twist him into something he was never intended to be—a vicious dog. They will purposely select ill-tempered, unstable dogs and breed them to dogs with similar temperaments. Their purpose, supposedly, is to develop a vicious guard dog or watchdog, or to extend their machoism by walking around with a "loaded gun on a leash."

Conversely to this philosophy, however, the best guard dogs are actually those with the *most* stable temperaments and the intelligence to know the difference between an attacker and an innocent stranger. The best guardians are also those with an intense desire to please their owners and obey their commands, even in unlikely circumstances.

Because of a few bad apples, however, Boxer owners should make sure they are model dog owners to prevent the potential of a city or state proposing a breed ban law that includes Boxers.

What You Can Expect from a Breeder

In addition to a scrupulously planned breeding program, really good breeders are very careful about the homes in which their puppies are placed. If you plan on purchasing a puppy from a quality breeder, you can expect to be questioned—in a friendly way, of course—about your lifestyle, your living arrangements, and your plans for the puppy, as well as whether you have the full support of your family members, if you have family. If you work during the day, the breeder will want to know who will be able to walk and feed the puppy when you're not around. The breeder will also want to know if you have a fenced backyard and whether you plan on making this dog an indoor dog or an outdoor dog. (The correct answer is an indoor dog with lots of supervised, outdoor playtime!)

In addition, a reputable breeder will most likely want you to come to his or her home and have your entire family meet some adult Boxers. The reason for this is for the breeder to meet you in person, and for you and your family to meet a group of nicely behaved adult Boxers. The key word here is "adult." Many times, dog lovers fall in love with the puppy without taking into consideration just how big and strong and jubilant an adult Boxer can be. Also, sometimes small children, though they are familiar with dogs and comfortable around smaller breeds, are intimidated or frightened by the Boxer's size. Additionally, an uncertain spouse may go the other way when he or she meets a Boxer "up close." The breeder knows that these potential conflicts are better addressed directly and resolved amicably before an exuberant puppy enters the picture.

Please don't be put off by the inquisitiveness or the "pre-reqs" of these breeders; they're not trying to be nosy or pushy, they're just trying to be sure that their puppies go to people who are going to be able to properly care for and raise the puppy. Reputable breeders know what it takes to raise a Boxer puppy and they are acutely aware of why Boxers fail in certain homes. They want to make sure that the recipients of their puppies are well equipped and ready to take on this job.

An added bonus of purchasing a puppy from a breeder who really knows what he or she is doing with the breed is that you will have a support network for life. You will be able to call this breeder with any question or problem and either be able to get

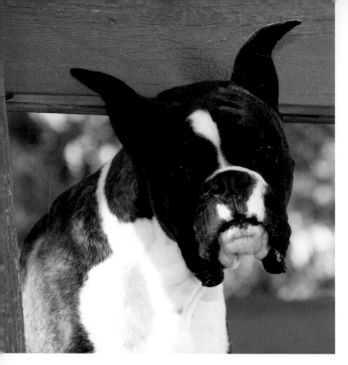

a good answer and sound advice toward solving your Boxer problem, or the breeder will know where and how to get the answer to your question. These folks have a wealth of information and enough cannot be said about how much support good breeders give to all of their puppy owners. For this great relationship to develop, however, you must be com-

Champion Bloodlines

Beware of want ads advertising "Champion Bloodlines." A large percentage of Boxer pedigrees will have a token champion many generations back—which means literally nothing. Parents and grandparents that are champions *are* champion bloodlines.

fortable talking with and consulting the breeder. If you have the impression that the breeder might think you're being tedious or may tire of your questions, you might consider another breeder. All of the breeder's vast experience is no help to you if you aren't comfortable communicating with him or her.

Beware When You Buy

Of the thousands of Boxers that are bred each year, it is safe to say that less than 25 percent are products of reputable breeders. The majority of registered (and unregistered) Boxer puppies are the result of what are called "backyard" breedings. These breeders, though perhaps well-intentioned, do not show their dogs nor do they compete in performance events. They haven't screened or certified their dogs for hereditary diseases, nor have they studied the genetic tendencies of certain hereditary traits. In most cases, they have a well-loved female Boxer and they want to have a puppy "just like her." The rest of the litter they figure they will sell to friends and neighbors, maybe advertise in the local newspaper, and perhaps even make a little profit.

You may be able to find a nice Boxer puppy from a neighborhood litter and the puppy will undoubtedly cost less than a puppy from a reputable breeder. Your chances of purchasing a puppy with health problems, however, are far greater with the backyard breeder than with one who has done his or her home-

Web Warning!

Many terrific Boxer breeders have beautiful websites, which are filled with helpful articles, tips, records of their dogs' wins and health certifications, announcements of upcoming litters, and of course, tons of beautiful photographs of their dogs. *Be careful!* Disreputable Boxer breeders—and often the very puppy mills you are trying to avoid—produce some rather slick websites advertising their Boxer puppies. (Some dishonest puppy sellers have been known to "lift" photos of beautiful dogs from *other Boxer websites* and post these photos on their websites!)

So, how do you know if what you're looking at is a bona fide great Boxer breeder with an established kennel... or something a bit shady? Here are some common red flags:

You might be looking at a "masked" puppy mill website if:

- The dogs are referred to by their call names with no registered names or titles provided.
- The dogs have not won any titles (e.g., conformation championships, obedience titles, working titles, etc.).
- The breeder does not list the health tests and certifications that he or she requires each dog to have before it is bred (i.e., OFA for hips; CERF for eye disease; ARVC genetic test, etc.).
- No mention is made of any local, regional, or national club membership.
- There is a health and purchase agreement/contract... but it is all to the seller's advantage.
- The breeder will ship a puppy anywhere to anyone, sight unseen, without meeting and talking to the buyer in great depth.
- Credit cards are gladly accepted.

work, has verified the health of the parents, and guarantees the puppies' health. Also, the backyard Boxer puppy is not the pup you'd want to purchase if you are considering competing in conformation; there won't be any show-quality puppies here. He also may not have the form or temperament needed to compete in many performance events.

Another important consideration is that since the backyard breeder is inexperienced, puppy owners will not be able to turn to this individual for advice and problem solving. And, because backyard breeders have no facilities to keep any dogs other than their own, they will not be able to—nor will they express a desire to—take back your puppy for whatever reason.

Again, this is *not* to say that a nice family pet Boxer can't be found from a source such as this. It just means that if you buy a puppy from an inexperienced breeder, it is a "buyer beware" sort of purchase. You may be able to select the pet of your dreams who lives a healthy and full life free of health problems. Or you could wind up with a puppy who has inherited every possible ailment known to dogdom and quickly rack up veterinary bills that far exceed the price of what you would have paid for a well-bred, health-guaranteed Boxer.

But there are worse sources for Boxers. There are Boxer breeders—and this term is used loosely—who use their dogs for profit only, period. Their goal is simply to produce puppies as a cash crop. Corners are cut, vaccinations are skipped, and little concern or thought is given to what dog is being bred to what dog and how that breeding might affect the outcome of the health, temperaments, and conformation of the puppies. Also, the dogs and puppies are kept in substandard conditions and have little if any positive interaction with people. These breeders then sell their puppies to puppy brokers who distribute the puppies to sellers around the country. Many of these puppies end up for sale in pet stores.

Though these puppies have been bred and raised in poor conditions, this is, again, not to say that you can't find a nice pet from this source. It's just that the cards are stacked against you for finding a puppy that is healthy in mind and body. Also, if you purchase a puppy from this source, you are supporting the puppy farmers' business. Not a very nice thought, is it?

How to Find That Great Breeder

Now that you know why you want to go to a really good, experienced breeder for your Boxer puppy, how exactly do you find this person? This is the hardest part. These breeders don't advertise their litters in local newspapers. If they do advertise their litters, beyond simply word of mouth, it is generally in publications, such as the breed magazine, the *Boxer Ring,* or perhaps on the breeder's personal web page. Despite the lack of publicity, these breeders often have their puppies sold even before they are born. Because of the reputation that precedes some breeders, there are those breeders who actually will have show, performance, and pet owners literally lining up for the expected puppies. In order to be sure of receiving a puppy from a litter, puppy owners are often required to make a deposit to reserve an unborn puppy.

Boxer rescue: At first glance, this doesn't seem to be a source for breeders; after all, these folks are rescuing unwanted Boxers, right? Yes, but did you know this group rescues puppies, too? If you don't want to adopt a Boxer puppy, these folks can still help. The American Boxer Rescue Association (ABRA) can be one of the very best places to ask for a quality breeder referral, since these rescue folks *know* which breeders take their dogs back and which don't. They also know who stands behind their breedings and provides positive support for their puppy owners. If you need to go out of your area to find a truly great breeder, your local rescue workers will be very frank with you and won't pull punches. If you want a puppy, ABRA wants to make sure you are directed toward a breeder who, in turn, will make sure you go into the endeavor with your eyes open and your feet well planted on the ground. Enough said. These people are tops. For phone numbers, websites, and e-mail addresses, see Useful Addresses and Literature, page 194.

United States Boxer Association: This national club focuses on the European and German ideal of the Boxer as a working and structurally correct dog. Members are active in agility, obedience, tracking, scent work (drug dogs), and *Schutzhund* competitions. The club also offers ZTP tests and European-style conformation shows. If you are looking for a Boxer with the intention of competing in performance events, a call to this organization would result in a list of more specialized Boxer breeders. See Useful Addresses and Literature beginning on page 193.

Dog shows: If you want to meet several breeders at a time and see a sampling of their dogs, attend a dog show in your area. You'll find a lot of breeders and owners sitting ringside before, during, and after the judging. This is a great opportunity to meet some fine Boxer people in your area, make some important contacts, and

learn a lot about the breed. You'll also quickly find out who has puppies or upcoming litters.

Another great place to meet and talk with Boxer owners at a dog show is far away from the excitement of the show ring. It's a place many lovingly refer to as the "RV Camp." This is where dog owners and handlers stay with their dogs during the day while waiting for their next event. Other than the time just prior to ring time, the atmosphere here is very laid back and quite congenial. You will find that most owners here will be more than happy to talk to you about Boxers in general and their own dogs. A stroll through this area can be even more fun than watching the judging.

Dog show listings: The American Kennel Club (AKC) lists upcoming dog shows on their website, as does InfoDog (*www.infodog.com*). These sites provide links to where you can search for dog shows with the listings organized by date and state. InfoDog provides an additional link to the sponsoring club's website, where spectators can get more information on the location of the show. Additionally, a week before the show is held, InfoDog posts ring numbers and times for each breed. This allows you to know exactly when Boxers will be judged, as well as how many dogs will be competing.

Local breed club: No show in your area anytime soon? Check with the ABC to see if there is a local Boxer club near you. If there is, you can call the contact person for this club—usually the secretary—and see if this person can direct you to a reputable breeder in your area. The names, locations, and contact information for ABC-member clubs can easily be found on the ABC website, too (see Useful Addresses and Literature, page 193).

All-breed dog clubs: In many areas, there may not be a local Boxer club, but there may be an all-breed club. Find out who the corresponding secretary is for this club and see if he or she can refer you to a few reputable Boxer members. These members may not be breeders themselves, but they may be able to point you in the right direction toward a top breeder.

Veterinarian: If you know a good veterinarian in your area, he or she could be a very good source for information about breeders. At the very least, your veterinarian will know which ones take good care of their Boxers and breed quality dogs. If you have a veterinarian, ask him or her to recommend a breeder.

Obedience clubs: If you have a training club near you, ask one of the trainers if he or she can make any recommendations for Boxer breeders. Good breeders strongly advocate obedience training Boxers, so if there's a reputable breeder in your area, the trainers in this club should be familiar with the individual.

Advertisements: Be wary of this source. Anyone can place a slick, color advertisement in a magazine but that doesn't mean he or she is a reputable breeder. Magazines have no criteria for breeders to meet, other than that the check for the ad space clears the bank. Some publications are better sources for dog breeders than others, and, as mentioned previously, the breed magazine, *Boxer Ring,* is probably the best known. Since this publication is geared toward show breeders, it reaches few pet owners, and advertisers are not trying to reach the mass puppy market. If looking in general interest dog magazines, be sure to read between the lines of the advertisements. If the ad touts "puppies all the time," avoid this breeder!

If the ad is *not* promoting championship bloodlines and dogs that are tested (and certified "clear") for hereditary diseases, be sure to question this aspect, if you call.

Finding a Puppy That's Best for You

Now you're at the fun point. You've found the breeder you want to work with and that breeder has a litter coming up. What do you do now? If you walk into the breeder's home and are faced with as many as six or more wriggly, bouncy Boxer puppies, how will you decide which one to take home? And, will your decision be the best one?

General Impressions

Take a look at the overall condition of the breeder's facility. Have the puppies been raised in the home? Have they been raised in a modern and clean kennel? Or are they in filthy conditions, exposed to the elements in the backyard or in a decaying barn? If you are looking for a puppy to be with your family, the puppy should come from a clean and loving environment. The breeder should already have made a concerted effort to expose the puppy to all facets of everyday life. If for any reason you are unhappy or uncomfortable with the premises or the overall condition of the dogs and puppies, leave immediately *without* a puppy. Your gut instincts will *not* lead you astray in this situation. Poor conditions indicate an irresponsible breeder.

Pick Your Purpose

One way to narrow the field is to decide ahead of time if there is a particular role you want your Boxer to fill. Do you want to get involved in dog shows? Compete in agility? Or are you just looking for a great pet? Deciding what you want can help you and your breeder select that perfect puppy.

Show: If you are interested in entering the competitive world of dog showing, you must find a puppy with wonderful conformation. The puppy must also be a great mover and possess that classic, irresistible Boxer temperament. Though many puppies in a well-bred litter may do reasonably well in the show ring and can pick up a few ribbons and perhaps a few points toward their championship, there are few puppies in the litter who will have what it takes to do very well in the show ring and finish a championship.

Among these elite Boxers, there are even fewer who will be able to rack up multiple breed wins, group placements, maybe even a Best in Show.

Knowing which puppy in a litter shows the promise of being a future champion (or more) is a mixture of skill, knowledge of the breed, and gut instinct. Many puppies who look terrific at 12 or 16 weeks do not turn out as expected. For this reason, some breeders may "hold" their potential show puppies until they are four or five months old (or older), when the breeder has a better feel for how the puppies will develop. Other puppies who look good but aren't considered "pick of the litter" have been known to develop beyond an owner's wildest dreams and succeed in the show ring.

A show-quality puppy is not a guarantee of a magnificent dog; it is the breeder's educated guess based on what the puppy looks like at an early age. The show-quality puppy may cost a bit more than the other puppies in the litter, but it is the only way to go if you plan on showing. Because there will be very few puppies in the litter that are show quality, you will have very few pups to pick from. In fact, you may simply be asked: "Male or female?" Or, maybe there won't even be a choice.

Note: Flashy dogs, with white markings on their legs, chest, and collar, used to be given reference over solid fawn or brindle Boxers in the show ring. In recent years, however, "plain" Boxers have been winning more and more. This is in large part due to a change in the Boxer breed standard that was enacted in 2005. The new standard points out that lack of flash is not a fault: "The absence of white markings, the so-called 'plain' fawn or brindle, is perfectly acceptable and should not be penalized in any consideration of color." So a Boxer that has tremendous conformation, temperament, and movement is competitive even with few or no white markings.

Performance/working: If you are looking for a Boxer who will be able to participate in performance events, you need to relay this information to your breeder, too. An experienced breeder can help direct you toward Boxers with temperaments that are most suitable for sports, such as a puppy that is eager to please, looks for human direction, and enjoys close companionship. The puppy will also need to possess a certain amount of athleticism and drive.

Companion: Though every Boxer in a well-bred litter should make a good pet, if you are interested only in having a great canine partner, then you don't need to consider his show potential. This puppy, though good-looking and bred for health and a good temperament, may not quite have what it takes to compete in the show ring. The flaw may be minor, and virtually unnoticed by anyone other than a serious Boxer breeder or judge, but it is usually enough to classify the puppy as "pet" or "companion" quality. The puppy's flaws are also those that make it unsuitable to be bred.

With a pet-quality dog, you can expect the breeder to require that you sign a spay/neuter registration. Or the breeder may only provide you with a Limited Registration, which means you can participate in many performance events, but cannot compete in the show ring. You will also be required to supply proof of spay/neuter to receive your registration.

Male or Female?

Many people mistakenly say, "I want a female," because they think a female dog is the sweeter of the sexes. With Boxers, this is not necessarily true. Some of the best snugglers and Boxers with the easiest-going temperaments can be males. If you're looking for the best temperament, don't limit yourself to one sex or the other; much like people, each Boxer has his or her own unique personality. If you already own a dog, however, and you want to introduce the Boxer puppy as the second pet, then you may want to carefully consider which sex puppy you choose.

As a general rule, fewer troubles tend to erupt with paired dogs of the opposite sexes. For example, if you already own a male dog, you will want to look for a compatible female. If your dog at home is a dominant type, you will also want to consider a less pushy temperament in the puppy. Boxers generally get along relatively well with each other, but many Boxer owners say that once a Boxer dislikes another dog, the grudge is forever.

Color

One thing the Boxer doesn't lack is color; brindles and fawns come in nearly every shade and hue imaginable. Some Boxers are "flashy" and have a lot of white markings; others are plain and have little if any white. Still others are pure white or "check," with spots of fawn or brindle. If you are looking for a show-quality Boxer, white markings are

not as critical as in past years. Judges are encouraged to judge plain Boxers on equal terms with flashy dogs. If you are looking for a companion dog or one to compete in performance events, any color goes. A word to the wise, however: With a companion dog, don't rule out a puppy with a great temperament if he is in a color other than your first choice.

Cropped and Docked, or Au Naturel?

Many breeders in the United States automatically have their veterinarians dock their puppies' tails and remove dewclaws shortly after being whelped, and crop ears between 9 and 12 weeks of age. If you do not want your puppy cropped and/or docked, you will need to discuss this issue with your breeder. Chances are that you will not be able to purchase an undocked puppy, simply because this procedure is done when the puppy is newly whelped. However, there may be room to negotiate with the Boxer's ears.

Alternatively, if you want to have your Boxer's ears cropped, make sure you consult with your breeder about which veterinarian to use for this procedure. The long show crops can be quite tricky and, if not properly cut and given appropriate aftercare for weeks and even months following the surgery, the ears may not stand up properly. To avoid a flop, literally, make sure you have the procedure done properly and make sure your Boxer puppy is in skilled and respected hands.

When You Meet the Puppies

Enjoy the moment. Hold the puppies. Play with them. Bask in the experience of being able to take part in puppy play without all the worries of puppy care on a large scale. It won't take long when visiting a group of pups before their individual temperaments begin to emerge and become apparent. Once you've gotten a bit of puppy play out of your system, you'll need to begin buckling down to the business of deciding which Boxer puppy will be the one for you.

An experienced breeder will be extremely helpful in helping you sort through the temperaments, conformation, and overall potential of the puppies. The more you know about this selection, the more assured you will be that you've selected the right puppy.

Temperament Testing

There are two temperaments that you'll want to avoid, if possible, in selecting your puppy:

1. The first temperament to avoid is the fearful puppy. An experienced Boxer owner who has a lot of time and patience may be able to take this puppy and calm his fears; however, a fearful puppy is not a good choice for an inexperienced Boxer owner. Fear biting is the number one cause of dog bites. Rearing a timid Boxer so that he is accepting of strangers, children, and new sights and sounds can be an enormous undertaking for the novice owner and is really best avoided, particularly for those with young families.

Note: An entire litter of fearful puppies indicates that the dogs have not been properly socialized by the breeder. These pups are best avoided since their mental condition shows a lack of concern from the breeder.

2. The second temperament that should be avoided by a novice or first-time Boxer owner is the very bold puppy that enjoys bossing his or her littermates around. This puppy could be showing some dominant tendencies that, though not insurmountable with appropriate socialization and training, could be too challenging for most pet owners. In other words, this puppy may, at maturity, try to exert his dominance over family members.

In most litters, the "middle" puppies are usually the best temperament choices. They are happy, playful, and neither timid nor pushy. This also is the group in which there is the greatest number of puppies from which to choose. From this group you'll want to find the puppy who enjoys being picked up without excessive wiggling, comes when you've got his attention, and likes to follow people when they walk by. All of these traits help to indicate a puppy who will enjoy human contact and will be an eager student in training sessions.

Physical Examining

When looking at a litter of puppies, it is important to physically handle them and look for signs of good health.

• The puppy's coat should be smooth and clean without any missing patches, which might indicate ringworm, mange, or a variety of unwanted skin conditions.

• Check the puppy for fleas and ticks; he should have neither.

• How does the skin look? Is it smooth, or is it bumpy or flaky and dry? Can you find any pustules, which might indicate an allergy or former flea or tick bites? Again, any deviation from the norm can be an indicator of ill health.

• Do the puppy's eyes look bright? Or are they weeping?

• What about the puppy's orifices? If you detect a discharge from any of these areas, this could indicate that the puppy is ill. If you happen to see the puppy relieve himself, diarrhea and/or blood in the stool is a red flag for worms, parvovirus, or giardia.

• Also, look at the puppy when he stands and when he is moving about. Does he appear to be symmetrical with legs of equal length? Does he move freely? If you are selecting a show dog, you'll need to pay particular attention not only to how the dog is put together, but also to how he moves. A great-moving Boxer commands attention.

Making the Selection

So many puppies, so little time! Though the task of choosing a Boxer puppy can be a tough one, the stress of making a decision can be reduced if you do your research and are prepared to make a decision by using some common sense. Usually, after a session with the puppies, there is one particular pup that catches your eye and your heart. (If one puppy does not stand out, come back later for a second look.) If this puppy has a great temperament, is put together well, and comes from a good breeder with a track record of healthy dogs, you should feel comfortable in your selection.

Note: Never take your children with you to select a puppy. The begging and pleading of children may pressure you to purchase a puppy that is not best for your family. Make the selection first and either bring the puppy home or bring your children back at a later time to pick up the new family member.

Now it's time to enjoy. When you take this puppy home, you "become" his mother, his littermates, and his breeder. You are the one he will look up to for all his needs and guidance. Take this responsibility seriously and your Boxer is sure to reward you with the best he can give you.

Chapter Five

Adopting the Adult Boxer

For those who find rearing a perpetual motion Boxer puppy a little daunting, or for those dog lovers who are interested in "doing the right thing," adopting an adult dog might be just the ticket. Or, maybe you're someone who wants to know exactly what you're getting before you buy it. These and many other reasons are given in favor of the argument for adopting an adult Boxer. If adopting from a Boxer rescue, you can be assured that the Boxer experts will match you with the best adult Boxer possible. However, be aware that most municipal pounds and many nonprofit shelters do not have the resources to provide extensive temperament testing and screening. If adopting a Boxer from one of these sources, it is highly recommended that you take an experienced Boxer owner with you to evaluate the dog, transport the dog in a crate immediately to your veterinarian for an additional evaluation, and then take the Boxer home, after he has been bathed, dipped, groomed, vaccinated, and spayed or neutered.

Benefits and Drawbacks

Yes, it's true: With an adult Boxer you miss the cute cuddly months. But you also miss the teething, chewing, house-training, crate-training, and many other aspects of puppy ownership. Of course, adopting an adult Boxer is not without its challenges, too. Most adult dog adopters, however, say that the benefits far outweigh the challenges, and relate that the experience is so fulfilling that they'll never go the puppy route again.

Note: It is estimated that 25 percent or more of all dogs in shelters are purebreds. Shelter workers relate that purebred dogs are often hard to place because they are viewed suspiciously by potential adopters. People tend to accept mixed breeds in shelters, but think that if a purebred is in the shelter, it must have done something really bad to be there. "Not so," say shelter and rescue workers. Most purebreds in shelters were impulse purchases as puppies by people who lacked either the abil-

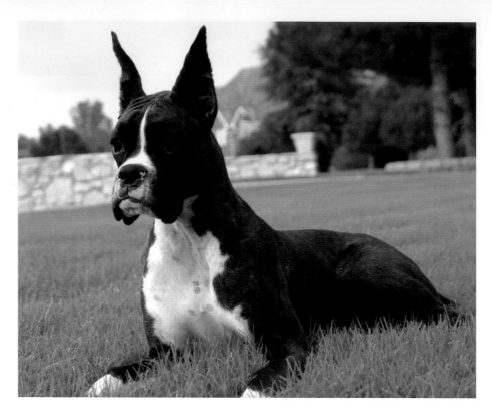

ity or the commitment to properly raise and care for the dog.

As one of the most popular breeds in the United States, Boxers make up a large share of these unwanted pets. Boxer Rescue estimates that thousands of Boxers are relinquished each year. Although Boxer Rescue itself places thousands of Boxers annually, many slip through the cracks.

Knowing What You Have

With an adult Boxer, what you see is what you get. There'll be no guessing as to whether that cropped ear will or won't flop over. Hoping

that those slightly cowed hocks will straighten up is a moot point with an adult: Either they're straight by now, or not. When you adopt an adult, you'll know exactly how your Boxer will look when he's an adult, because he is an adult.

With an adult dog, you will have the ability to know what types of diseases he may or may not have inherited before you commit your heart to owning the dog. Mature dogs can be tested for some heart problems, degenerative spinal diseases, deafness, vision problems, and hip and elbow dysplasia. Other health problems that often go unde-

Purebred Alternative Listing (PAL)

You've adopted a purebred Boxer and want to compete in some of the AKC's performance events, but your rescued Boxer doesn't have any registration papers. In other words, you have no proof that your Boxer is a purebred. What do you do?

Apply for a Purebred Alternative Listing (PAL) number from the AKC. With this number, your Boxer will be able to participate in most AKC events, such as agility, tracking, and obedience, but conformation classes are off limits to PAL dogs.

In order to receive a PAL number, the Boxer owner must fill out an application form, provide clear side, front, and back photos of the dog, and supply proof of spaying or neutering. A check must also accompany the application (call the AKC to find out the amount). The AKC reviews the photos and the application form, confirms that the dog looks like a purebred Boxer, and then issues a PAL number. This number is good for most competitions for the life of the dog.

The AKC also introduced a new program in 2009 that allows Boxer mixes to participate in a variety of performance events. The AKC's Canine Partner program is a great opportunity for those who have adopted a Boxer mix and want to compete in obedience, agility, or rally. The process simply requires filling out an application, providing proof of spay/neuter, and a small registration fee.

For more information on how to apply for a PAL or Canine Partner number, call the AKC at (919) 233-9767, or visit the AKC's web page.

---

tected in younger puppies, such as skin problems, allergies, and epilepsy, already should be evident if they are present in the adult dog. Instead of playing a wait-and-see game with a puppy, with an adult dog you'll have the ability to find out whether he has any serious health problems.

In addition to knowing how your adult Boxer looks and being able to screen for many serious diseases, you will also be able to determine the dog's temperament and his activity level. If you are looking for a Boxer who is a bit calmer and less active, you may be able to find this combination with an older adult Boxer. If you went with a puppy, you may have to wait eight years before your Boxer is "less active."

When you adopt an adult dog, you'll also be able to tell whether this dog has developed into a Boxer with the abilities and aptitude for any competitive canine sports. Adopting an adult dog takes the guesswork out of how trainable your Boxer will be when he hits adolescence or maturity.

Avoiding Puppy Problems

Chewing: Another advantage to adopting an adult dog is that a mature dog has already passed the teething stage. This is not to say that your adult Boxer won't love to chew, or that he won't destroy a piano leg given a chance. It just means that as an adult, your Boxer won't go through a period of the awful, insatiable desire to gnaw on everything in sight as his adult teeth erupt. With appropriate toys and supervised activities, an adult Boxer may have significantly fewer problems with chewing than a teething puppy on a toothy, seek-and-destroy mission.

House-training: Still another puppy challenge that can be avoided when adopting a mature Boxer is house-training. With puppies, there will always be at least a few accidents before the puppy gains control of his bodily functions, starting around four months for consistent control. With an adult Boxer, the bodily control situation is already covered, and, many rescued Boxers already know to do their duties outside; in some cases, no house-training is needed at all. Imagine that! For some owners, that benefit is worth the ticket right there. Adult dogs who aren't already house-trained can be quickly trained using a crate and careful supervision. As one adopted dog owner exclaimed, "It took *months* to house-train the puppy, and two days to train the adult."

Speaking of training, old dogs *do* learn new tricks. The desire to please his owner does not diminish with age. Adult Boxers are eager learners. Because of their age and maturity, they are more focused and can concentrate for longer periods of time, making training sessions go much faster. Remember, half the battle with training a puppy is simply getting the pup's attention for more than a nanosecond. With lots of positive reinforcement and a few yummy treats, even a Boxer who is untrained and is considered a "handful" can quickly be roped in and developed into a model citizen.

Challenges of the Adopted Boxer

It would not be fair to say that adopting an adult dog is *not* without its challenges. In many cases, the adult Boxer transitions quickly into his new home and becomes a beloved pet, but in other cases, a more experienced owner may be needed to help undo some of the damage done by the previous owner, and the transitioning from rescued Boxer to family Boxer takes some creativity, patience, and time.

Not Knowing

Perhaps the biggest challenge in adopting a rescued Boxer is "not knowing"—not knowing how the Boxer was raised as a puppy, or what types of things he is quirky about. For example, one rescued Boxer suffered from severe separation anxiety. The owner discovered this fact when he left the Boxer unattended while he walked to the mailbox. When he returned a few moments later, the Boxer had torn the drapes and blinds off the window facing the mailbox. Another Boxer had a previous gunshot injury that no one knew about until the dog was touched in the "hot" or formerly tender spot. The dog didn't bite, but she let out a yelp that startled everyone.

Fortunately, if a Boxer is placed through a branch of the ABRA, he has been thoroughly examined and temperament tested by both an experienced Boxer breeder/owner and/or a veterinarian. The Boxer is fostered by a member of the breed rescue program to further determine if the dog has any fears, quirks, or oddities that might catch a new owner by surprise. When the Boxer is fully assessed, he is then considered ready for adoption.

Health Headaches and Heartaches

Adopting an adult Boxer can be an expensive veterinary adventure. When a Boxer is unwanted enough that his owners are willing to drop him off at a shelter, the dog frequently has been medically or socially neglected and, in rare cases, physically abused. Many rescued Boxers come from homes where they were poorly fed and are very

thin. Their coats are so brittle from malnutrition that it literally falls out as they walk. It can take months to bring a dog back from this condition, and even longer before he regains healthy skin and a glossy coat.

Some rescued Boxers have received little if any veterinary attention. Most need worming. Some have flea infestations that are so severe the dogs are deathly ill when they enter the rescue program. Heartworm is rampant in many areas of the country, and untreated Boxers in these areas are almost always infected. Depending on the age and health of the dog and the degree of the infestation, the Boxer may or may not be treatable.

All of these conditions can create some rather costly veterinary bills and require extensive attention and care from the owner. For the most part, however, if the Boxer comes from a rescue organization where the dog is screened and treated for health problems, the adoptive owner is aware of the dog's condition prior to adopting him. Many times, the rescue has already provided for the dog's veterinary care and has covered this cost, too. So, even in cases in which it may be very expensive to bring the dog back into good shape, the owner enters into this canine venture completely aware of the situation.

Bigger Issues

When a fully grown dog relieves himself inappropriately in the house, it's a bigger accident to clean up than that of a small puppy. (Crate-training is still a must with adults!) And, when a 60-lb. (27-kg) Boxer decides to chew, instead of finding a puppy-size mess, such as a shredded pillow, you may come home to find the whole couch ripped apart.

Training an untrained adult Boxer can be a bigger issue than working with a small, wriggly puppy, too. Training a happy, strong dog can quickly turn the "walking nicely on a leash" exercise into an arm socket-wrenching drag around the block.

Fortunately, however, there are solutions to all these problems—with a little patience, ingenuity, and determination, there is hardly a problem that can't be overcome in time.

Adult Dog Sources

Just as the quality of a puppy can vary greatly with the quality of the breeder, the quality of the adult dog adoption depends on the organization handling the adoptions. In other words, there are many sources for great adult Boxers. The success of the placement, however, depends largely on the evaluation skills of the "rescuer" and the policies of the organization regarding adoption.

Boxer Rescue

The most highly organized rescue network for Boxers is the ABRA. Founded in 1982 by Boxer breeder Tracy Hendrickson of Tulsa, Oklahoma, as an independent rescue, the ABC pledged its financial and membership support in 1989. Today, ABRA is comprised of a national network of experienced Boxer breeders, owners, and admirers of the breed who are willing to devote their time and energies to rescuing Boxers. ABRA has representatives in nearly every state who actively rescue Boxers of all ages.

The reason that Boxer Rescue is such a tremendous source for adult dogs is the thorough job these people do when placing a Boxer, and because of the network members' vast experience with Boxers. These people live, breathe, and know Boxers. They can quickly judge a dog's temperament and know exactly what type of owner and what kind of home would best suit the dog.

Every dog is thoroughly evaluated for temperament and health, spayed or neutered, and treated for any health problems *before* being placed in a new home. Many dogs are fostered with volunteers who not only help nurse the dogs back to health, if necessary, but also work with the dogs on basic life skills, such as simple commands and house-training. With few exceptions, no Boxers are placed into permanent homes until they are considered to be good companions and, if they've been ill, are recovered or well on their way to recovery.

This organization even finds "special" homes for "special" Boxers. For example, older Boxers who have a few minor medical problems and perhaps an ache or pain here or there are often placed with older humans who appreciate the gentleness of these older Boxers and can relate to having to take a few meds for various minor conditions. Boxer Rescue also has puppies from time to time who are available for adoption.

If you can't adopt an adult Boxer, there are still many ways you can support Boxer Rescue.

1. Foster homes: People are always needed to temporarily house rescued Boxers.

2. "In-kind" donations: Contact your local rescue to find out what kinds of supplies are needed, such as food, collars, leashes, blankets, or crates.

3. Cash donations: These are always appreciated.

4. Other special skills: Newsletter writers, photographers, and those who can help transport Boxers from shelters to veterinary offices are just a few of the volunteer services that may be needed, and appreciated, in your area.

Adopting from Boxer Rescue: What to Expect

Boxer Rescues operate a bit differently from the typical pound or small nonprofit shelter. Though the process may seem a bit involved, it all runs fairly smoothly. Rescuers remind us, too, that this careful process is necessary to find good, permanent homes for the rescued Boxers.

Application/screening: The first stage in adopting a Boxer is filling out an application form.

The application is usually divided into two sections: personal background information and what you are looking for in a Boxer. The personal background information includes questions regarding who lives with you and their ages, what your experience has been with dogs and other pets, what types of pets you own now, how you intend to keep your Boxer—indoors, of course!—and why you are interested in adopting a Boxer.

The second half of the questionnaire deals with the specifics of what qualities you are looking for in your next Boxer, such as color, male or female, age range, AKC registered or not, and any special abilities (such as the ability to perform in agility, obedience, or rally).

When you're filling out this application, do yourself, the rescue, and the potential Boxer a favor—be honest! Don't answer falsely just because you think your true answer is not the one the rescue wants to hear. Rescues want their Boxers to go to good homes, but they also know there are no perfect owners nor perfect homes. These rescues are looking for people who are willing to make changes, if necessary, to their homes and yards and alter their lifestyles in order to satisfy the needs of the dogs. For every potential sticking point, there is a viable solution, if the owner is willing to be a little flexible. So, be honest. Your sincerity not only will gain you the trust of the rescuer, it will also help the rescue to pair you with the best Boxer match possible.

Once you've completed and submitted your application, you will receive a phone call from the rescue. It is perfectly OK to call them to confirm that they received your application. These folks can get very busy with rescues and they wouldn't be human if an online form or e-mail wasn't sometimes temporarily buried on a desk or counter for a few days.

When the rescue calls, it will be for an informal interview. The rescuer may have a few questions regarding how you answered some questions. For example, if you said your yard wasn't fenced, the rescue may want to know when you plan on putting up your fence. Or if you have a fence, the rescue may want to know what type of fence you have and how tall it is. You can expect more detailed questioning on your previous pets and even how they died. If you have children, the rescuer will want to know their ages, their attitudes toward animals, and if they've had any experience with dogs.

If all goes well here, you will either be approved and put on the waiting list for a suitable Boxer, or you may be asked if a representative of the rescue organization can come by for a home visit.

Home visit: A home visit doesn't necessarily mean that the Boxer Rescue doesn't trust your answers. If they thought you were a "front" for a research laboratory, you wouldn't have gotten even this far. Many rescues visit the applicant's home as a matter of course. It allows them to meet the prospective owner and family where they are most comfortable—in their own home. It also allows them to see any potential problems and suggest solutions to rectify the situation.

The rescue visitor often brings a Boxer with him or her for the family to meet. If the adopter is not single and has a spouse and/or children, it is important for the rescue organization to see the support of the dog adoption made by every family member. As is true of many things, the dog adoption is only as strong as its weakest link. If you have a spouse who is lukewarm about adopting a Boxer, the spouse's apprehensions need to be addressed immediately and resolved *before the Boxer is adopted.* The rescue coordinator's experience and advice can help calm many trepidations and provide reasonable solutions for some concerns; however, the final balancing act is within the family.

Waiting list: You've come a long way, and now you've got to wait. Adopting a dog is not like purchasing a puppy, where you know when the litter will be available and can select the exact date on which you bring your puppy home. With dog adoption, it's a wait-and-see option. You wait while the rescue sees if it has a Boxer that will suit you well. Depending on your lifestyle and other factors, Boxer Rescue may already have the "right" Boxer waiting in a foster home. Or it may be a month or more before the "right" Boxer arrives. Since the rescue has no way of knowing what Boxer it will be rehoming next, it's often impossible to guess just how long your wait will be. Remember: The waiting list is not first come, first served. Each dog is matched with the person that the rescue thinks is best for that dog. If you are the type of person who could do well with a wide range of Boxers, have a home that can immediately accommodate a dog, are experienced training dogs, and aren't picky about the color or sex of the dog, you will probably be called before the harder-to-fit applicants on the list.

Rest assured that when Boxer Rescue gets in a dog it thinks might be a good match, you *will* get a phone call. You will be asked to come visit the dog at his foster home. Often, the matches are right on and it's love at first sight. However, if the dog isn't what you expected, tell the rescue. If you're somewhere in between—for instance, you wanted a fawn female and this is a brindle male—the rescue may suggest you take the dog home for the weekend and see how you feel. By Sunday afternoon, you may find that rescue knows best and you wouldn't part with your Boxer for the world. On the other hand, the weekend visit may confirm your concerns about a particular dog.

The key to a good match is keeping an open mind toward the adult Boxers you are presented, remembering that many of the cosmetic issues, such as poor coat or thinness, will remedy themselves as the Boxer begins his life of good food, exercise, and care. Also, keep an open line of communication between you and the rescue. This is the dog you will be caring for during the next eight or more years. It should be the one you want and the one that brings that zany Boxer joy into your life. Make sure the match is right.

Contracts and papers: Once you've found your bouncing canine pretzel, you're not through yet. There is a bit of paperwork you should receive and a contract that must be signed before you can take your Boxer home.

You should receive a copy of the dog's veterinary work, detailing vaccinations and wormings, verification of spay/neuter, and results of any tests, such as a blood test for heartworm. You may also receive a copy of the dog's information sheet from its previous owner, detailing the reasons for the dog's surrender. You may not be able to see the transfer of ownership paper, but you should have the presence of this document verified. The transfer of ownership prevents the dog's former owner from trying to reclaim the dog at a later date.

As for contracts, the one you will sign may have several stipulations in it. The first is that if you are unable to keep the Boxer, or if your care is not satisfactory, Boxer Rescue retains the right to take back the dog. There may also be a clause in the contract that requires you to keep your dog on a leash while outside or in a safe, fenced yard. Again, violation of this stipulation could cost you the dog.

The contract will contain a clause that limits the liability of the rescue. This clause says that you, the adopter, agree to hold the rescue harmless of any damages the adopted dog causes. If your adopted Boxer shreds your favorite couch one afternoon, you cannot hold Boxer Rescue liable for the replacement of the couch. Basically, this clause is the "it's-your-dog-now" clause that places the responsibility on you for the dog's actions.

Follow-up visits: Once you have your adopted Boxer, you won't be left hanging. Boxer Rescue is similar to a big family. Rescue volunteers will check on you from time to time to make sure your Boxer is adjusting well to his new life. If you have any questions regarding care or training,

these people are the folks to ask. Their sincerest hopes are that you and your Boxer are partners for the life of the dog. They will go to all ends, it seems, to make sure they are there for you.

Additionally, you'll find the rescue family is a bit of a social group. Many local rescues hold annual picnics and other activities where everyone brings their dogs, eats, plays games, and has a really fun time. Some rescues print newsletters that are sent to all adopters to keep them informed of the rescue's goings-on and upcoming events. It's a great group to be associated with, and it's also great fun for your dog.

Keeping tabs: If you adopt a Boxer from rescue, don't forget to send your local group a photo of your happy Boxer in his new home. Nothing makes a rescue happier than knowing their Boxers are doing well. Many rescues keep scrapbooks of their rescues—and most remember each dog *by name*.

Breeders

Though few people consider consulting with a breeder for dogs other than puppies, a quality breeder may also be a source for an adult Boxer. Occasionally, a breeder may have an adult Boxer who had been reserved for the show ring or a performance event and the dog just didn't turn out according to the breeder's expectations. The dog is older and not a puppy, so it is not as easy to find a home for him. Mind you, this dog is probably a knockout as far as looks, because he is considered an "almost" show dog.

Since this dog grew up with a quality breeder, he has been properly socialized, habituated to everyday living and certainly car travel, and trained beyond just being a "good" dog. This Boxer will be calm and still for baths, toenail trimming, ear cleaning, and veterinary exams. He will also walk on a leash with little pull—in the show ring dogs are not allowed to pull their handlers around—stand rock solid when given a *stand* or *stay* command, and will allow total strangers to check his teeth, legs, and body, just as a judge would do in the show ring.

The breeder's adult dog will also have been fed a quality diet, and, depending on his age, he may have been screened and certified "negative" or free (hopefully) from several diseases. The breeder's adult Boxer will not come without a price, of course, but you can see the many advantages to obtaining an adult dog from a source such as this.

The breeder may also have another type of adult dog available. If the breeder stands behind his or her breeding, the breeder will take back any Boxer who he or she has bred for any reason and at any age. This includes Boxers who are suddenly without a home because of the owner's death or perhaps a divorce. Dogs are sometimes returned because their dander is discovered to be causing serious allergies in the owner's new baby. Since quality breeders really try to screen their prospective puppy owners very closely, most dogs are returned for good reasons. These dogs are generally fine family pets who have had some training and most likely are house-trained. The breeder knows the dogs' history and temperament well, so there isn't much guesswork involved in evaluating them.

Again, a quality breeder's adult dogs can make great pets—perhaps even potential show dogs. There have been recorded cases where a returned dog developed into something exceptional and the new owner finished a championship and campaigned the dog as a special quite successfully.

A word of warning: Not all breeders are quality breeders (see Chapter Four). Purchasing an adult dog from a less-than-reputable breeder could mean a whole pack of trouble. Puppy farmers sell off old brood bitches when the poor things can't produce puppies anymore. These dogs have been caged and socially isolated most of their lives. This dog can be exceptionally difficult to turn around. It is best not to purchase such a dog.

Shelters and Pounds

This is the time-honored way of adopting an adult dog—through your local city pound or area humane organization. Depending on the services provided by your area shelters and pounds, your experience trying to adopt a Boxer from these facilities can be either marvelous or less than memorable.

The ideal shelter or pound offers a comprehensive evaluation of the dog's health and temperament when he enters the shelter and doesn't rely on the surrendering owner's questionnaire answers. One would assume that the dog's owner would want to make his or her dog look like the ideal canine citizen in order to increase the dog's chances of being adopted. Shelter officials say, however, that the opposite is true; owners frequently write down that their dogs are impossible to house-train or have aggression problems *just to give themselves a "good" reason for turning in the dog.* If you are looking at a Boxer in an adoption facility that doesn't evaluate the dog's temperament, be sure to take a trainer or an experienced Boxer breeder with you to properly evaluate the dog.

As for the dog's health, there are shelters and pounds that offer extensive veterinary services, including spaying or neutering before the dog leaves the facility. The dogs are also wormed, vaccinated (if the dog has no vaccination record), and tested for heartworm prior to the adoption. Contrast this to shelter facilities that do not have the funds to perform these services and simply release the dog "as is" for a sum of money.

Some nonprofit shelters even offer dog ownership counseling services, require some screening of potential owners, and provide training classes for new dog owners. Municipal pounds generally can't afford these luxuries and focus their attention on treating the dogs humanely until they are either adopted or euthanized.

The key to remember when adopting a dog from a shelter or pound is that before you bring the new dog into your home, have a professional trainer, experienced breeder, or veterinarian evaluate the Boxer's temperament. If the dog looks like he will be a good pet, then, before you take him home, schedule a complete veterinary checkup, a spay/neuter (an overnighter), followed by a visit to the groomer. This way, you can bring home a clean, vaccinated, and altered Boxer that is ready to begin his new life.

Don't forget the crate! Yes, you already love your newly adopted Boxer, but he must earn your trust. On the way home from the shelter or pound, be sure to crate your Boxer. There have been stories of usually peaceful dogs going berserk in the car and nearly causing an accident. Also, you don't know if the dog will get carsick or not, or if he is perhaps suffering from intestinal distress. Avoid problems and crate the Boxer in the car.

If you visit a shelter or pound several times but don't see any Boxers, there may be a reason why. Many of these facilities work in concert with local Boxer Rescues. In these shelters and pounds, when a Boxer is surrendered, the facility immediately calls an official with the Boxer Rescue in that area. The shelter or pound knows the dog will be well cared for and placed in a good, permanent home, and the shelter will then have the room to take in another dog. This cooperative rela-

Dog Bites

• How common are dog bites? An estimated 74.8 million dogs live in homes in the United States. Each year, more than 4.7 million Americans are bitten by a dog, with an estimated 800,000 of these incidents requiring emergency room treatment.

• Who gets bitten? Mostly children. The vast majority of those bitten are children under the age of 12.

• Who's doing the biting? Not strays. Not feral dogs. Studies indicate that the dogs doing the biting are *owned* by someone. Many of the bites are sustained by family members from the family pet.

tionship benefits Boxer Rescue, too, in that rescue volunteers don't have to check the shelters and pounds on a frequent basis for Boxers and can spend their time in more productive areas, such as placement activities.

A Word on Kids and Dogs

Unless a Boxer has been severely mistreated or unsocialized with children, these dogs generally make wonderful family pets. Their temperament is downright silly at times, and the more a child wants to play, the more the Boxer will play. The greatest danger with Boxers and children is the potential for this exuberant, muscular dog to accidentally bowl over a smaller child. They tend to be very forgiving and seem to have a high threshold of pain (in case a child falls on them).

No dog, especially if not well known by the owner, *should ever be left alone with children.* If you cannot closely supervise your Boxer with your children, then you must be able to separate them. If you cannot separate them, then you should not have a Boxer. With any adopted dog, you must never assume anything. You must make the dog *prove* he can be trusted. And your children must prove to you that they know how to treat a dog kindly and with respect.

Remember, you didn't raise this dog from puppyhood. You don't know its life experiences. You do not know everything about this dog's past. Most importantly, you do not know his threshold for biting. The power and shape of the Boxer's jaws make a bite from this breed a near-guaranteed trip to the emergency room. So, even if you've adopted the sweetest Boxer in the world, don't take anything for granted around your children.

Teach your children the following rules around the Boxer:

1. Don't pet a dog while he is sleeping. Wake him first by calling his name.

2. Respect the dog's crate. This is his special area and is not for children.

3. Do not pet the dog while he is eating or try to take a bone away from him.

4. Don't roughhouse with the dog.

5. Be kind to your Boxer and he will be your closest companion.

Chapter Six

Preparing for the New Arrival

Whether you are adopting an adult Boxer or purchasing a puppy, you will need to prepare your home and family as best you can. Since Boxers really never grow up—they just get a little gray—both future adult and puppy owners need to make sure their homes and yards are safe for the new arrival. Because the Boxer is quick and agile, and don't forget clever, this job can be a little more involved than perhaps with a more complacent breed.

Preparing your home and taking a proactive stance in Boxer care can be the single best way to avoid much of the stress of introducing a new dog or puppy into the home. It will cut down on the possibility for much of the destruction associated with an active puppy or inquisitive adult, and the structure will help the dog or puppy to settle into his new life even quicker.

What to Do in Advance

There are two things you must do well in advance of picking up your new Boxer: schedule an appointment with your veterinarian, and register for training classes.

Veterinarian

If you are purchasing a puppy, make sure to schedule the veterinary appointment on your way home from the breeder's, if possible. If this isn't possible, make sure this appointment is made within three days at most, even if the breeder says the puppy isn't due for any vaccinations and has just been wormed. The reason this first appointment is so important is that you want your trusted veterinarian to give you a very honest evaluation of the condition—both physical and mental—of your puppy. You also want your veterinarian to give the puppy a complete and thorough health exam before you take him home. Thus, if your veterinarian detects any serious health or temperament problems with the puppy, you will know this immediately and may decide to return the puppy before you've passed the point of no return with your heart. Also, if you have other animals or dogs at home, it is important to make sure the puppy is not harboring any communicable diseases.

This first visit to the veterinarian is very important with an adult Boxer, too, especially if the dog has been adopted from a shelter or pound with very few services available to adopters. Even if you have received your dog from Boxer Rescue, the veterinarian should be your first stop on the way home. As mentioned previously, if you've adopted an adult from a shelter or pound, your second stop, after seeing the veterinarian, should be the groomer so that your Boxer is free of ticks and fleas and smells good.

Along with a physical exam, if you are adopting an adult Boxer, this is the time to get your dog spayed or neutered. Unless your Boxer is particularly weak and needs some rehabilitation, or your veterinarian suggests delaying the procedure for another reason, get it done now! You will be able to pick up your Boxer the very next day and begin a wonderful life together.

Training Classes

One thing that many new puppy and adult dog owners forget in the excitement of bringing a new Boxer home is the importance of registering for a training class *before the dog comes home.* Puppy preschool or kindergarten classes fill up very quickly and are generally offered in cycles of six or eight weeks. If you miss the chance to sign up, you'll have to wait until the next training cycle. This could be the difference between training a small 12-week-old puppy and working with a strapping 5-month-old Boxer.

Note: When considering a young puppy training class, be sure to discuss with your veterinarian the risks of contracting a deadly disease before your Boxer puppy has been fully vaccinated. In some areas of the country there are higher risks of disease outbreak than in others. Additionally, it is important to ask about the training school's protocol as far as vaccination requirements (all puppies should have "x" number of vaccinations in their puppy series prior to enrollment) and how well the facility sanitizes the floors immediately before and after the puppy class (a cleaner should be used that kills any potential viruses or bacteria that may have been shed by adult dogs).

If you're adopting an adult Boxer, it is equally important to enroll in a basic or beginner's obedience class. Even if your Boxer is well-trained, it is important to begin a training class to develop a close relationship with the dog and to confirm—or reconfirm—who is the leader and who is the Boxer. If your Boxer has had little training or has some behavioral challenges, beginning a training class and working with a professional trainer becomes even more important.

Whether you are purchasing a puppy or adopting an adult dog, you'll find that a solid course of training will help deepen the bond between you and your Boxer, as well

as provide you with a support group for all sorts of training and non-training questions.

Supplies You Will Need

You've set up your appointment with the veterinarian and have a space reserved in the next training class; now it's time to make sure you have all the supplies you'll need for your new Boxer. If you're lucky, you live in a town with a pet store that never closes, so if you forget something or discover you're running low on a critical dog product, you can run out to the store and get what you need. However, it's really a good idea to plan ahead so that for the first few days you can enjoy your new pet and not worry about running back and forth to the store for supplies.

The following is a basic list of supplies most commonly needed in those first few days and weeks of new Boxer ownership.

Collar

Your Boxer will need a collar when you bring him home from the breeder or rescue. Do not buy a choke chain or any other collar that functions as a choke for your puppy or adult's "everyday" collar; in most instances, you will not need this type of collar even when you are training your Boxer. A collar like this is guaranteed to catch on something and strangle your dog. Boxers have been known to strangle themselves on their collars in the "safety" of their own crates.

If you are purchasing a puppy, an efficient collar is one that expands over several sizes. Your puppy will grow by leaps and bounds in his first year and will go through several collar sizes before he is fully grown. With an expandable collar, you can keep adjusting it as your puppy grows. You'll want to be careful, however, to make sure that the collar is properly adjusted and fastened so that the excess collar is firmly held in place and does not create a choking hazard.

Flat-buckle collars are good choices for both puppies and adults and can be purchased in nylon, a tough cotton web, and leather. Though leather collars are generally the gentlest on the dog's coat, they are a bit more expensive and seem

to be considered a particularly attractive snack or chew item among both puppies and adults. If your Boxer chews through a cotton web collar, you may be less upset than if he devours a pricier collar, so if you are purchasing a collar, it may be more economical to purchase collars of less expensive materials while your puppy is growing and save the expensive collar for when he is fully grown.

Leash

Your Boxer should always be walked on a leash. Even very young puppies should be kept on a leash when they aren't in a protected, fenced backyard. Though they look small and appear to want to stay very close to you, there is no way you can catch one of these little guys when they decide to take off. If they dash about and run into the path of an oncoming car, you will never forgive yourself for your negligence. *Buy a leash.*

With that said, there are several options when it comes to leashes. The simplest is the standard 6-ft. (1.8-m) leash with a snap attachment that hooks to the dog's collar. Leashes come in nylon, heavy cotton web, and leather.

Beyond the standard 6-ft. leash, another popular favorite is the retractable leash. This leash extends as the dog pulls. It can also be "locked" at a certain length. Until you have your Boxer trained to walk nicely on a leash, this probably is not the best leash to have. If your Boxer is zinging in and out at will, you won't be able to teach him to stay by your side. Even in the locked position, the hard plastic container and handle for this leash is a bit bulky to hold. The leash is wonderful, however, if you want to allow your Boxer a little freedom. For example, if you are going to the beach for a walk and you want to let your dog splash in the waves without having to go in yourself or allowing him off leash, a 30-ft. (9-m) retractable leash is perfect. If you purchase this leash for your dog, be sure to buy the grade for heavy or very strong dogs. If you buy a cheaper, lighter-weight version, your Boxer may very well hit the end, break the leash, and keep going.

Crate

This is something you just can't do without. You will need a crate for traveling in the car, and you will need a crate to safely confine your puppy or new adult when you can't be at home to supervise him. Crates are also very helpful in teaching house-training manners (see pages 174–175), so the question is not whether to purchase a crate, but which crate to purchase and in what size.

Size: If you're adopting an adult Boxer, you'll have no problem deciding what size crate to get; since you know the exact size of your Boxer, you don't have to guess the size of the crate. The crate should be big enough for the dog to stand up, turn around, and lie down comfortably.

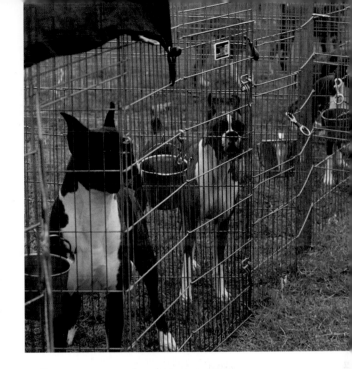

If you are purchasing a puppy, you can only guess what you will eventually need. What the puppy fits today, he will not fit in the next month or two. A crate that fits the puppy and is not too big often helps to expedite the house-training process. Boxers prefer to be dry and clean and will prefer to "hold it" than to be near a mess. When using a crate of this size—not overly big— the owner must be very vigilant in heeding the puppy's need for frequent and regular relief. If using an adult crate, many styles offer partitions that can be fastened in order to make the crate just the right size. Regardless of your setup, the puppy should not be in the crate for more than 8 to 10 hours during a 24-hour period.

To figure out what size crate your puppy might eventually grow into, ask your breeder his or her opinion. If your puppy is a larger male, he may eventually need a large crate. If you are selecting the runt of the litter, he may never outgrow a medium crate; then again, he may grow a lot while in your care and require a larger crate. Don't fuss too much over this issue. The worst situation is that if you err on the small side, you will just have to buy another crate.

Type: The type of crate you purchase can be important in helping your new Boxer settle into his new life. Crates generally come in two styles: wire and plastic. The wire crates are very open and have a metal pan at the bottom that can be layered with sheets of newsprint and a thick layer of shredded newspaper for a puppy, or a soft pad for an adult who doesn't chew, shred, or fluff when he is bored. The advantages to this crate are that it can be folded up into a compact space when not in use, and its airiness makes it cooler on warm days. One of the disadvantages of this type of crate is that because it is so open, some dogs and puppies do not feel comfortable or protected. Also, they tend to be a bit more expensive, particularly if they are collapsible and have a coating that is not dangerous to dogs and prevents rusting. This type of crate is not approved for shipping on an airline, either.

The hard-shell plastic crates, however, are approved for shipping via air cargo, so if this is ever a remote pos-sibility, you've got this angle covered without having to purchase another crate. The solid plastic crates also give a dog a more protected, denlike feeling because they have no wire mesh except for the door to the crate and a few side ventilation panels. These crates can be lined with paper for puppies, or a fitted pad or soft blanket for the adult who behaves well in a crate. The disadvantage to the plastic crates is that they are not as airy as the wire crates and there-fore do not provide as much air circulation. They are a bit warmer in the winter than a wire crate, and are quite a bit warmer in the summer. As long as your crate is in a cool spot in your home, this shouldn't be a problem. Another consideration with this type of crate is that it doesn't collapse for storage if you no longer need it on a regular basis.

Of course, there are also designer crates that are beautifully handcrafted to look like end tables or other pieces of furniture. These crates are completely functional and can be custom-made to the owner's liking. They do, however, come with a price—so it might be best to wait to order one of these beauties until you are sure your Boxer pup or adopted adult dog is over the chewing stage.

Pet Gates

If you plan to limit your Boxer's activities to one easily cleaned room that contains little of anything of value that can be destroyed, you will need a way to safely contain your puppy or adult in this area. Pet gates come in a variety of styles and heights and can either be permanently attached to your wall—be sure to find the studs and not just the drywall—or temporarily attached using pressure to lock them into place. There are some gates made in "extra tall" that are nearly double the height of a regular gate. They are made to expand to a variety of different widths, but be sure to measure the area you want gated to make sure the style you choose will work in that area.

Identification

Dog owners often forget that one of the most likely times for a dog to get lost is when he first comes home. Puppies have no idea where they are or how to find their way back home, and adults in a new area will be equally confused if they get lost. Before you go to pick up your new Boxer, make sure to have a tag made that is engraved with the following: "I am a Boxer," followed by your address and mobile number with area code. The area code is important because adult dogs can travel miles out of the area in a relatively short time. The mobile phone number should be used so that if you are traveling and your Boxer gets loose, anyone who finds your dog can call you while you are in the area. Additionally, even if your Boxer is missing in your neighborhood, it is quite likely that someone will call you *while you are out of the home looking for your dog*. The

mobile number works wherever you are and at all times. Once you've brought your puppy or adult home and have decided on a name, you can have a new tag engraved with the Boxer's name and other information. You may also consider putting "Reward" on the tag to encourage finders to call. Then you need to consider a permanent means of identification, either through tattooing or microchipping.

Tattoos: When people tattoo their dogs, they aren't talking about getting a picture of a poodle etched onto the chest of their Boxers. And you don't have to go to a tattoo parlor to get the service done. Tattooing pets as a means of permanent identification is growing in the United States. Tattoo registries report phenomenal rates of recovery when a pet is identified by a tattoo. The procedure is relatively painless; the dog doesn't even have to be anesthetized. Tattoos can, however, fade with age or get "stretched" as a puppy grows, to the point that they are illegible. Tattoos are best for near-adult or adult dogs. The number should be registered with a national registry and the dog should wear a tag that says "I have a tattoo" with the phone number of the registry engraved on the tag.

Microchips: Microchips are about the size of a grain of rice and are implanted between the dog's shoulder blades. This is a veterinary procedure and, according to implanters, is only momentarily uncomfortable when the chip is injected under the skin. Each chip has its own code and when the dog is scanned with a chip reader, the number will pop up. Shelters across the country have scanners and many use them regularly. The problem with chips right now is that the average person who might find your dog would never know that your dog was chipped, or perhaps even what microchip identification is. If you live in an area in which chipping clinics are provided by the area shelters and your shelters do, in fact, scan for these chips, this might be a good option for your dog. But be aware that in some instances the chip can travel under your dog's skin to a place where a scanner won't pick up the presence of the chip.

For further information on tattooing and microchipping, your best source of information is your veterinarian, who can discuss additional pros and cons of each form of identification and help you make the best decision for your Boxer.

Newspapers, Old Towels

Start collecting newspapers now. Forget the recycle bin; your very own personal little recycler is on his way. You'll need plenty of fresh papers to line the Boxer's crate for quite a while.

Go through your linen closet and pull out any towels that are wearing out. Your Boxer won't mind if they have a few holes in them or aren't super plush, as long as they're cuddly. Towels are easier to wash than expensive pads or crate liners, and they can be pawed and tugged at until they have been molded into a suitable little bed. If you find your Boxer is a shredder, however, stick to newspaper and leave your stash of towels for baths. A puppy or adult dog who shreds towels is very likely to swallow bits or entire strips of the towel. This can lead to either choking death or an impaction. It's always better to be safe than sorry, so if you line the crate with towels, *watch your Boxer carefully!*

Food and Bowls

Your Boxer needs to eat. Be sure to ask the breeder or rescue what type of food your Boxer is accustomed to eating and purchase a sizeable bag of this food. If you plan to change over to a different food, wait a week or so and then begin mixing parts of the new food in until the transition has been made (see Nutrition, pages 133–137). Of course, you'll need bowls for both your dog's food and his water. Heavy non-tipping bowls are best and tend to minimize cleanups after meals. (They also discourage your Boxer from galloping around the backyard with a food bowl in his jaws and using it as a major chew bone.

Treats

Gotta have some treats. You'll need these primarily for training. Prepackaged treats can be high in salt, sugars, and preservatives, which when used in quantity or over time could cause gastrointestinal distress. Many owners who are seeking a more healthful alternative may prefer to offer their Boxers bits of cooked liver (grill it outside and it won't smell up the house), chopped chicken baked with garlic, or for the weight-conscious Boxer, bits of chopped carrots can serve as an excellent training treat. Treats should be chopped into small pieces so that you can reward your dog often throughout the day without stuffing him.

Toys, Toys, and More Toys

Your puppy or adult Boxer will need a lot of toys; Boxers live by the credo: "I may have to grow older but no one said I had to act maturely!" You will need to be careful in purchasing appropriate toys for your puppy or adult. Because the Boxer has a very powerful jaw and "bite," and because he *loves* to chew and rip and tear at his toys, the toy must be virtually indestructible. It must also be big enough that it can't be swallowed or have pieces that might break off that could be swallowed.

There have been entire articles written on what types of items have been removed from the stomachs of dogs. And finally, the toys must be large enough that the puppy or adult cannot try to swallow it and choke on it instead.

So do not give your Boxer stuffed, soft toys. The innards can be swallowed, which can choke or impact the dog. Don't give your Boxer tennis balls *unsupervised*; it's okay to play *fetch* with a tennis ball but always retrieve the ball at the end of the game. ER veterinarians have removed more tennis balls from dogs' stomachs than you could ever imagine. Do choose toys that are made for large, heavy chewers. Many manufacturers are now producing dog toys expressly for dogs such as the Boxer. Read the labels carefully and use some good judgment. If in doubt, never let your Boxer have the toy unless you are carefully supervising him.

Anti-chew Salve and Sprays

These concoctions are made by several manufacturers and come in a variety of nasty flavors. The purpose is to use this substance on things you don't want your Boxer to chew on in your home. For the most part, it's effective, except with Boxers who lack taste. Check your pet-supply store.

Stain and Odor Removers

There will inevitably be a few accidents, so it's good to have a supply of pet stain and odor remover on hand to immediately attack any indiscretions your Boxer may have on your carpeting or furniture. A lot of progress has been made in this product market, and there are now stain and odor removers that actually do their job! Look for products with no perfumes or odors, or products whose odor disappears when the enzymes or microbes finish breaking down or eating the residue. Also, seek out products that are safe for dogs; many of the newest products contain no surfactants or dangerous chemicals and break down into substances that are completely safe for humans and dogs.

Grooming Brushes, Nail Clippers

While you are warming up that credit card with all the other pet store purchases, you might as well invest in a nice set of grooming supplies. A good natural bristle brush and toenail clippers should do it for now.

Purchases for You

Now that you've invested a small fortune in supplies for the new Boxer, what else is there to buy? Fresh batteries for the camera is one purchase you shouldn't forget. Puppies grow quickly and rescued adults rehab rapidly. Be sure to have a fresh memory card (or two or three) and a ready camera to capture those photo moments.

Also, read up on as many books on puppy care and training as you can get your hands on. Books focusing on puppy problems are useful in that they give you a "heads up" as to potential problems in your home. A few favorite books are listed in Useful Addresses and Literature (see pages 196–197).

Boxer-proofing Your Home

To keep down the level of turmoil a new Boxer can bring as he charges into your life, you'll want to take some precautions in your home. The purpose for this is twofold: You'll want to limit the potential destruction a puppy or adult can inflict on your home furnishings, and you'll want to safeguard your Boxer from hurting himself.

Electrical cords: Get these out of sight and out of reach. If your Boxer

gets his teeth on an electrical cord, he will either pull over a lamp or chew through the cord and can kill himself. If he partially chews through the cord, you now have an electrical fire hazard. For cords that can't be hidden, try a plastic runner designed specifically for cords on flooring or, if the cord is in a visible spot, you could apply a no-chew product that is foul tasting but harmless.

Shoes: Puppies and adults don't know the difference between their toys and yours. Therefore, your shoes, clothes, briefcase, television remote, and other items that you may be used to leaving around the house are fair game for chewing. Anything you don't want your Boxer to turn into a canine toy should be kept out of reach of your Boxer.

Counter patrol: Jumping on the kitchen counter is a snap for a full-grown Boxer, or even an adolescent. Boxers have a tremendous sense of smell—they can be very good at tracking and are used as drug-sniffing dogs—so don't think your dog won't notice that box of fresh donuts on the counter. Nor should you ever believe the innocent, pious look your Boxer gives you as he rests peacefully on his bed. As soon as you leave the room, the donuts will be his!

Garbage lockout: So many people complain, "My Boxer is driving me crazy! He's always knocking over the garbage can and strewing garbage everywhere. What can I do to get him to stop this?" This one has an easy solution: Put the garbage away. Do not leave it out for your Boxer to eat. It's not good for the dog, and it's probably not good for your blood pressure. If your Boxer learns to open the cabinet doors to the garbage can, bungee cord them shut if you have to, or move the receptacle to a room with a door and firmly shut the door.

Table decorations/breakables: The Boxer is a joyful, exuberant dog. Love your Boxer for this and, to avoid the heartbreak of some cherished memento crashing into a zillion little pieces, move your breakables to higher ground. Maybe this is the time to splurge on that curio cabinet you've always wanted.

Upholstered furnishings: Before your Boxer joins your family, decide in advance if he will be allowed on the couches (because he will surely ask), and if so, which couches are allowable and which aren't. To avoid having a hairy couch, put a pet throw or an easily washed blanket on the couch. Also, remember that not all Boxers can be trusted to sleep peacefully on a sofa when no one is watching. Left unattended, a Boxer can wreak havoc in a very short time.

Carpets: Until your Boxer is completely house-trained, it is a good idea to limit his carpet time to only that period just after he has relieved himself, and while he is being closely supervised.

Deadly Everyday Products

Many everyday consumer products are poisonous if consumed in even small quantities by your puppy or adult dog. These products have child-safe packaging; however, child-safe is not Boxer-proof! Here are some products that should be kept away from your Boxer.

Toilet cleaners/fresheners: Blue water is not healthy for your dog to drink. And, since it's a given that a Boxer will drink from the toilet if the seat is up—even if there's a fresh, cool bowl of water set out—make sure there's nothing in the toilet water that could jeopardize the health of your dog. Toilet bowl cleaners that release chemicals with every flush are not a good idea around dogs. If you feel you must use these products, keep the lid down at all times and the door to the lavatory firmly shut.

Roach motels/pesticides/rodenticides: These products contain some serious chemicals that should always be kept away from your puppy or dog. It won't take much of these products to kill a Boxer. The products also seem to be attractive in taste and smell to dogs, so don't count on your Boxer leaving the little roach motel alone behind the couch. If creepy crawlies or mice are a problem in your home or yard, you will need to consult with your veterinarian and a professional exterminator for advice on how to handle the situation.

Cleaning liquids: Don't assume that because you keep your floor, counter, and bathroom cleaning fluids under the sink and behind closed doors that these products are squirreled safely away from your Boxer. If your Boxer figures out how to open your cabinets, or if you leave these products out, your Boxer could be in very serious trouble. Make sure the cabinets containing these cleaners are either up high where the Boxer can't get to them, or behind doors that can't be opened by the dog.

Medicines: Prescription and over-the-counter medications should be kept out of reach of your puppy or adult Boxer at all times. This includes such innocuous products as medicated shampoos, toothpaste, and sunscreens. None of these products were designed to be eaten.

Antifreeze: It only takes a very small amount to leak or spill from your car, and your Boxer will die if he laps the fluid up. This product is very poisonous and has been the cause of many dogs' painful deaths. Be careful!

Boxer-proofing Your Yard

Your home is not the only area you will need to prepare for the new arrival; you will also need to Boxer-proof your yard. The most critical aspect here is to have a safe fence. Not only do you need to have a fence to keep your dog in, but also to keep other dogs and people out.

Liability on a Chain

A dog chained to a stake in an open yard is not an acceptable means of keeping a dog. A chained dog is not only at risk of choking but he is socially isolated, too. When socially deprived, even an even-tempered Boxer can develop into a frantic and perhaps aggressive animal. A dog such as this is no plea-sure to own and is, in fact, a liability. If another dog or a child crosses your property within range of the staked dog's chain, and the dog has developed a bad attitude, the safety of those crossing your property could very well be in jeopardy.

If the city or state has a danger-ous dog law, the owner of a dog who bites is held accountable for that dog's actions. Depending on the city or state laws, owning a dan-gerous or vicious dog can result in heavy fines and jail time.

Fences

What type of fence is best for your Boxer? A tall, sturdy one would be one good answer. Both wooden privacy fences and heavy chain-link can work well in a backyard. Which style you choose depends on your tastes, the size of your pocketbook, and what the fencing restrictions are in your neighborhood. Boxers are athletic, and, if determined, can scale seemingly impossible fences. They can also dig under a well-built fence, so make sure that the fence extends flush with the ground to hopefully discourage any escape artist efforts by your dog.

Hidden electrical fences that work in concert with a collar are effective to a point. While your power is on, the fence is operational. If your power goes out, during an electrical storm, for instance, your fence is now "down." Your Boxer is probably gone, too. Another disadvantage to consider with this type of fence is that it allows other animals and people to come into your yard—something you do not want!

If you have an existing wood or chain-link fence, be sure to walk the entire length of it looking for loose or protruding nails, missing boards, or torn wire. Make repairs now before your Boxer accidentally injures himself. Also, invest in a padlock for your gate. Someone who knows how friendly your Boxer is may be tempted to steal him. A padlock may not prevent a theft, but it will help to discourage it. It also will help to discourage children from opening and perhaps not shutting your gate, letting your beloved Boxer loose.

Poisonous Plants

Many common annuals, perennials, bulbs, shrubs, and even trees are poisonous to dogs if eaten. Some plant poisons cause a minor irritation; others can kill your Boxer with just a small taste. Your veterinarian should have a complete list of toxic plants that you can keep as a reference. If your dog or puppy eats a plant and you're not sure what the plant was or if it is toxic, take whatever part of the plant you find, along with the dog, to the veterinarian's office as soon as possible. It's better to be safe than to have a severely ill or dead dog.

Animal poison control center: The American Society for the Prevention of Cruelty to Animals (ASPCA) maintains a comprehensive website (*www.aspca.org/pet-care/ poison-control/*) that includes a wealth of information, including a searchable database on toxic and nontoxic plants. Additionally, the ASPCA maintains a poison control

emergency call center operated 24 hours a day, 365 days a year: (888) 426-4435. Pet owners are advised that if the service is used, a $65 consultation fee will be charged to a credit card.

Pools

Do you have a pool in the backyard? Some Boxers enjoy a dip; others don't. If your Boxer enjoys swimming and you are going to allow him in your pool, make sure he knows where the steps are to get out of the pool. Dogs have drowned after jumping into a pool for a swim and then not knowing how to get out.

If your Boxer doesn't enjoy swimming, and you can't show him how to safely exit the pool, make sure he can't get near the pool. Keep him outside the pool's fenced area as you would any unsupervised child. Accidents do happen, and generally when you're not looking. One slip while running around the pool could drown a Boxer or a young pup.

Prepare Your Family

If you live alone, the only person you need to prepare for the new Boxer is yourself. If you are married, however, live with a roommate, or have children or older parents in the same home, you will need to have a "family talk" to clearly outline which family members will be charged with which chores. In addition, you'll want to make sure everyone understands which rooms the puppy or adult Boxer is allowed in and which rooms are forbidden—and decide now whether the Boxer is allowed on couches and chairs or not. And, learn what types of snacks are allowed and what types will upset your Boxer's stomach. Rules on shutting doors and gates may need to be revisited with younger children, and you should have a serious discussion about how to treat a dog kindly. In a home with multiple owners, cooperation and consistency are the keys.

Kids and Chores

What is the right age to give a child the responsibility of caring for and owning a Boxer? The answer is: It depends on the child. If a child must be reminded to brush her teeth at night or to take a bath, this child

cannot be expected to remember to feed the dog without supervision. With children under the age of 13 or so, direct parental involvement is necessary for the welfare of the Boxer.

Older teenagers may very well be responsible enough to care for a puppy or an adult Boxer, but parents will find that they still need to "be there" for the Boxer. Teenagers have pretty active lives with after-school practices, club meetings, and social lives. Your teen may very well be capable of caring for a dog, but may not be at home to perform all the chores, all the time.

Young children should never be expected to care for a dog by themselves; however, teaming with a parent can make a great learning experience and give you, the parent, precious "together" time with your child.

The bottom line with children and their responsibility is that to have a successful pet in the home, the parent must take an active role in the dog's care. This may mean keeping an eye out when your teen feeds the Boxer, or it may mean actively reminding your ten-year-old to freshen the dog's water every day. If a parent is not willing to be the underlying force in the raising of the Boxer, then now is not the right time to have a dog. Wait until you have the time and desire to participate.

Schedule Time Off

Your home, yard, and family are ready for the new arrival—but are you? Make sure you are well-rested before the Boxer arrives, because you may not get much sleep for the next few days. If you can, schedule the pickup of your puppy or dog so that you can visit the veterinarian and have him back home for the weekend. Better yet, if possible, why not take a week off from work so that you can be with the Boxer and help him adjust to his new lifestyle? That way, if you're up at night because your puppy is a bit upset about leaving his littermates or, in the case of an adult, everything is just so new, you'll need the days off to catch up on your sleep.

Ready, Set, Go Get That Boxer

Once you bring that puppy or adult Boxer home, there's no looking back. You're ready, you're educated, and you know what your commitment level must be to make this relationship work. You've made all the necessary preparations to set your Boxer up for success in his new life. Without a doubt, you're ready to pick up your Boxer and begin a memorable and treasured canine-human partnership.

Chapter Seven

The Boxer's Life Stages

While it takes humans 20 years to reach physical maturity, a Boxer puppy will mature in just 18 months. The road to maturity is filled with adventure. As your puppy matures, he will go through several milestones in his physical and emotional development. The path is not always smooth; there will be a few bumps in the road, if only to keep the Boxer owner on his or her toes. With a good understanding of how your puppy develops and an awareness of the critical stages through which the puppy will pass, the Boxer owner increases his or her ability to raise a socially responsible adult Boxer who is a sheer joy to live with.

Prenatal

The puppy begins his life as a tiny speck developing in his mother's uterus. It will take roughly two months for the embryo to develop into a fetus that is ready to be born. During this development period, it is critical that the Boxer mother is well cared for both physically and emo-

tionally. Prior to breeding, the bitch should have been screened by a veterinarian for a variety of diseases and conditions that could affect her ability to conceive and possibly affect the health of her puppies. In addition, the prospective mother Boxer should be up to date on her shots and recently wormed. While the puppies are developing, her nutritional requirements increase, and experienced breeders are careful to make sure the pregnant dog's needs are met.

A healthy Boxer is not enough, say researchers, in developing healthy puppies. The treatment of the pregnant mother and her emotional state during her pregnancy has a strong influence on the future social abilities of the puppies. Imprinting, it appears, begins *before the puppies are even born.* In one study, it was shown that petting and stroking the mother had a significant effect on the puppies' future tolerance to being touched. A conscientious breeder, therefore, can facilitate the *good* attributes in his or her puppies. This is one more reason that it is critical to be very selective in choosing a breeder from which to purchase your Boxer puppy. Likewise, keeping his breeding stock isolated in a cage under marginal conditions in a "puppy farm," with minimal human contact, can have detrimental effects on the ensuing puppies. A poorly kept, stressful mother will transmit, to some degree, her poor physical and emotional health to her puppies.

Neonatal

When the puppies are born, they are totally dependent on their mother. Weighing less than a pound, their eyes are not open, and, though this theory may be reversed with future research, newly whelped puppies are thought to have limited capabilities of learning. They react to the scent of their mother's milk, know innately how to suckle, and can cry, whimper, and growl. Being physically near their mother is important in keeping the puppies warm.

Newborn puppies have limited mobility in these very early days and move by dragging themselves around. An exceptionally large litter—more than seven puppies—may require the assistance of the breeder through supplemental bottle-feeding of some puppies to make sure all of them are getting enough to eat. Bottle-feeding puppies is an arduous chore but must be undertaken if a mother is having problems with her milk supply or if she develops a mammary infection.

Puppies who are eating well and are healthy can be expected to double their birth weight within eight to nine days. The puppies' "milk" teeth also appear during these first few days.

In countries where docking is legal, the puppies' tails are severed by a veterinarian around the third or fourth day of life. At this time, if the puppies' dewclaws—the fifth toe located on the inside of each front leg—are to be removed, the veterinarian performs this procedure, too.

The Young Puppy: Two to Sixteen Weeks

By the time the Boxer puppy is two weeks old, his eyes are open and within a few days he will be able to see pretty well. At three weeks, the puppy can hear. Getting around is still a bit of a challenge for the little pups, but this skill is something these puppies will conquer quickly.

During the early weeks, the Boxer puppy begins to learn what it's like to be a dog. By being around his littermates and mother, he learns the rules and limits of play. Puppies who are removed from their litters too soon—before they are seven weeks old—will suffer mentally and, as a result, it can be difficult for an owner to overcome these handicaps even with extensive training. Studies indicate that puppies who are removed from their mothers and littermates at six weeks are not submissive to adult dogs, a dangerous thing for a puppy. Puppies separated at an early age also show abnormal behavior as adults in other studies.

Though puppies are commonly sold at eight weeks of age, many breeders will not release their puppies until they are 10 or 12 weeks old to assure the puppy has received the socialization he needs to begin his life.

This is also a critical time for the puppy to learn about humans. Experienced breeders gently handle their puppies throughout the day to begin and reinforce their trust in humans. Some research indicates that daily handling and picking up of puppies actually works toward inhibiting dominance aggression. The complete influence of handling during these early months is not totally known, but without a doubt, frequent handling and affection from humans helps Boxer puppies begin their development toward becoming loving canine companions.

During a puppy's first three months, it is critical to expose the puppy to as many friendly people as possible. Lack of human contact often creates unnecessary fear, wariness, and even phobias of people. The puppy should be introduced to all types of people, of all ages, and in a variety of settings, so that it doesn't fear a particular segment of the population, such as men, children, or people in uniform. This job begins with the breeder, and, depending on when you bring home your new Boxer puppy, as much as a month of this early socialization period is in your hands.

Contact with Other Dogs

Socialization with friendly, well-trained, and vaccinated dogs is also important while your Boxer puppy develops. Contact with unvaccinated and potentially sick dogs should be avoided. Remember that your puppy has not been vaccinated enough at this point to prevent him from contracting a deadly virus. Don't risk the health of your puppy. If you know of a healthy, even-tempered dog who is up-to-date on his shots, then some playtime for your puppy would be good. Once your veterinarian feels that your puppy has been properly vaccinated (between 12 and 16 weeks) and that he is not at risk among other dogs, you can begin puppy preschool classes where your puppy will be able to interact with several other puppies in a safe, controlled environment.

The first few months are not easy with a puppy, but they are rewarding. If you've done your job right, you will be well on your way to achieving a devoted, intelligent, and entertaining canine companion.

The Middle-aged Puppy: Four to Eight Months

When a puppy nears 16 weeks, an amazing thing happens—bladder control! This is exciting news for puppy parents who anxiously are awaiting more control from their puppy, just as parents anxiously await giving up diapers. Now, this doesn't mean that a four-month-old puppy won't have any more accidents, and it doesn't mean you can trust him on the carpet. What it does mean is that your puppy may not dribble across the floor when he becomes excited. He may also be able to sleep comfortably for eight hours without having to get you up for a 2:00 A.M. relief walk. In many ways, this age marks the beginning of a puppy who is truly growing up.

On the bad side, along with a gain in bodily function control also comes a loss of the puppy's milk teeth and the emergence of new adult teeth.

Teething Terror

There is probably nothing that will prepare you for this stage. Boxers are big chewers anyway, and the annoyance of new teeth coming in makes them, well, chewier.

- Make sure you have plenty of safe, indestructible chew toys for your dog.
- Discourage inappropriate chewing by not allowing anything within your puppy's reach that you don't want shredded or eaten.
- For those inanimate objects that you can't remove from your Boxer's chewing path but still can't stand to see destroyed, such as the cabinet corners or doors in the kitchen, or a table leg or two, spray or apply a harmless but foul-tasting formula specifically designed to discourage puppy chewing. Pet stores stock a variety of such products, as does your veterinarian.

Toys

"I want it! I want it!" No, that's not a toddler in the aisle of a toy store; it's your Boxer puppy begging for more stuff. Can you spoil a puppy with too many chew toys? Are you overindulging him if his toy basket runneth over? A resounding "No!" In fact, if you can buy at *least* 15 indestructible toys for your puppy, keep 10 out at all times, but rotate which toys you "hide" each day. With an ever-changing supply of toys to play with, your Boxer will be less likely to grow bored.

However, not all dog toys are created equally, and not all are safe for the mighty jaws of a growing Boxer puppy. When looking for suitable toys, here are a few things to consider:
- Balls can be swallowed. Buy only those that are too big to fit in your

dog's mouth. Watch as your puppy grows, too. Balls that were too big to swallow last week may choke your Boxer this week.
- Look for breakable parts. Chew toys should not break off into pieces—ever.
- Avoid toys designed for small breeds. Cute little toys that are soft and have squeakies are not meant for a dog who has the jaws to hold onto a man's arm and not let go. Puppies will quickly rip these apart, and then swallow the offending squeakie.
- Pull toys are fine to use with Boxer puppies if boundaries are set. Allowing a dog to win at tug-of-war is confidence-building and just plain fun for the dog. You do, however, want to be able to give the Boxer the *out* command (swap a yummy treat for the toy and say "out" as the Boxer releases the toy) so that he willingly releases the toy when playtime is over. In this way, you can engage your Boxer in a great game, but still maintain leadership by having him obey your command to release the toy. If you have a Boxer that tends to be possessive of toys, doesn't want to give up the tug, or tends to be a dominant dog who will push the limits (and perhaps try to intimidate you into leaving him alone with his toy), choose a game or toy other than tug toys.

Training

Training a puppy who is four to eight months old is not difficult if the puppy has already been receiving training since he was very young (eight to 10 weeks). In fact, some aspects of training can become easier because the puppy is more mature and his attention span is longer. An unruly puppy at this age— one who has received no training— can be a handful, but don't despair. He is still very trainable and within a matter of a few weeks, he will be recognizing several commands.

The puppy's socialization with humans and dogs should not stop; owners should continue to introduce their Boxers to as many people and "things" as possible, using the *sit-stay* (see pages 170–171) and having strangers offer the Boxer treats. Owners who have no young children or who live alone should seek out children. A Boxer lives up to his reputation of being good with children only if he is exposed to them constantly in a positive way. Make sure your Boxer is a role model.

Problems in socializing: If you are socializing your dog well and are actively enrolled in training classes, you should have few problems with your Boxer, but not all Boxers are perfect, and not all trainers are qualified to counsel owners who have dogs with behavior problems. You may need to seek the additional advice of a certified expert, such as a veterinary behaviorist or an applied animal behaviorist. The following are some red flags to watch out for with your growing puppy and are reasons to seek help immediately to prevent a more serious confrontation.

• Growling, snarling, or barking at all new dogs
• Barking, growling, or cowering at strangers (humans)
• Snarling or baring teeth when given a command or when touched or held by the collar
• Aggression toward other family pets, including other dogs and cats

The Adolescent Boxer: After Eight Months

Beginning at the age of eight months, your Boxer puppy will enter his "teen" years. Basically, this means you will have an adult-sized Boxer with a puppy's energy

level who is beginning to experience a wide range of hormonal urges. That high-energy puppy who ricocheted off your walls for the past few months will still have a tremendous activity level, but now he will weigh up to 40 or 50 pounds (18–23 kg) *and* he will be gaining muscle bulk daily.

In other words, you'll have your hands full. Remember all that training you've done for the last six months? Be prepared for your adolescent Boxer to suddenly find ways to "untrain" himself. Watch out for stubborn streaks. And, keep your eyes open for attempts to reestablish the order and rank within your canine (and sometimes human) household. This is not to say that your Boxer will suddenly become vicious when he becomes an adolescent; it just is a warning that you'll need to keep up the good work with your Boxer and continue to mold him into a good canine companion.

If you haven't trained your Boxer consistently by the time he reaches adolescence, what are you waiting for? It won't get easier. *Do it now.* The number one reason dogs are turned in to shelters is because their owners didn't take the time to train them. A trained Boxer is a joy to live with. An untrained *adolescent* Boxer is out of control. This is a very happy breed with lots of love and enthusiasm for everyone, but if you can't contain your Boxer, he may frighten or hurt someone with his sheer enthusiasm. He is not a tall dog, but he is a strong dog. If you aren't experienced training Boxers, or if you are particularly small or not very strong, you may want to consider hiring a trainer to get your Boxer going in the basics and then have the trainer train *you* on what he or she trained your dog. Once your Boxer learns the basics, you'll breathe a big sigh of relief.

Note: Boxers are an active breed, particularly as puppies; however, they are by no means "hyper." A hyperactive dog is one that is so frenzied that he *cannot* focus for any length of time. Training the hyper dog is frustrating, if not impossible. The Boxer, on the other hand, may be *active,* but he has the mental capacity to focus on what you are teaching him. He also has the desire to please you.

Spay or Neuter

Something you will need to consider when your Boxer reaches adolescence—or before—is the decision

Fact
Of the dogs that have been killed by cars, as many as 85 percent are intact (unneutered) male dogs.

to spay or neuter your dog. Unless you intend to be involved in showing or performance events and want to eventually breed your Boxer, it is in the Boxer's best interest, and yours, to have this surgery performed.

Males: A problem that compounds the Boxer's teen years is the surge of hormones that can course through a young male's body. Unless you are active in showing and might consider breeding your Boxer at a later date, your Boxer should be neutered by the time he reaches six months. An intact male can be a challenge to own. If there is a female within a mile that is in season, your wannabe stud will climb any fence and dig any hole to get to her, resulting in a litter of unwanted puppies. An intact male also can be much more aggressive with other dogs than a neutered male.

If you own a Boxer as a pet, or if you purchased a dog for showing or performance events who didn't quite measure up or has some hereditary defects or diseases, neuter your dog. You'll save yourself a lot of headaches and you'll decrease the risk of certain cancers for your dog. Neutering will *not* make your male Boxer a wimp, nor will the dog hold this procedure against you.

Females: An unspayed female will attract every male in the area when she comes in season. A female who is in season can also provoke terrible battles between unneutered male dogs who see themselves as possible suitors. She also has a hard time keeping herself clean during this time and can be a mess to clean up after around the house.

By spaying your female Boxer, you will spare yourself the headache of her coming into season. You may also very well extend the life of your female if you have her spayed, since uterine cancers and other female reproductive diseases can be avoided this way. Mammary cancer is also reported to be lower in spayed females if the surgical alteration is performed before the dog's first heat cycle.

Spaying and neutering are one-time procedures. They are performed so routinely by veterinarians across the country that owners should have few qualms (if any) about electing to have their pet altered.

All Grown Up

Most Boxers reach their full maturity by 18 months; some perhaps are late bloomers at two years. With proper preventive veterinary care, a sound diet, plenty of socialization, consistent training, and lots of love, your Boxer should develop into the outstanding companion he was bred to be.

The Silver Boxer

As much as we wish our devoted Boxers could live forever, they don't. In fact, a Boxer who has reached his seventh birthday is considered a geriatric—or a silver Boxer. (Silver is in reference to the silver or white hairs that grow in and around the Boxer's muzzle and eyes.)

With the aging process also come several changes in the Boxer himself. Owners who want to keep their older Boxers healthy and comfortable for as long as possible are advised to keep an eye on the following life changes in their dogs.

Lower Activity Level

For those owners who have been wishing that their active Boxer would just slow down, this is the time. Even if you don't wish your Boxer would become less active, he usually will. Without any other changes than activity level, however, your Boxer will gain weight and may become a rotund couch potato. Excessive weight at any age is not good, but with a senior, those extra pounds can place increased stress on the dog's heart and joints. In other words, a lot of fat is not good—for dogs or humans!

To prevent this from happening to your aging Boxer, there are several approaches that can be taken. One is to exercise your dog. When you no longer have a bouncy Boxer *begging* you to take him for a walk, many times owners *don't* take their dogs on walks. Make sure you can moti-

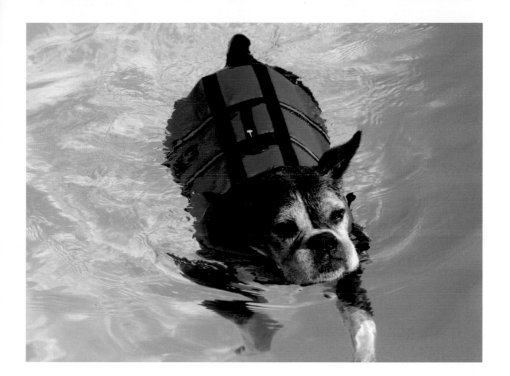

vate your senior Boxer to exercise. Walks are always good, as are "self starters," those Boxers who will take any excuse they can think of to play. Often, a playful dog will get an older curmudgeon to play. If not, better beat the pavement with your Boxer—it's good for you, too. Keep the exercise fun and gentle, and at a pace your older Boxer can enjoy.

Another approach is to cut back on your dog's food. Feed your dog only enough food to provide all the necessary nutrients and keep the right amount of weight on him. If you can't stand those pleading eyes after you've fed your pet and he has licked the bowl clean from its smaller portions, ask your veterinarian if a special diet designed for seniors might be more appropriate for your Boxer. A senior diet should be highly palatable (taste good) and be highly digestible. Some dogs have difficulties digesting their food when they age and don't absorb all the necessary nutrients. If the food is easily digested, your Boxer has a greater chance to absorb the things he needs.

Perhaps, however, the best approach is to use both methods: gentle exercise and a reduced diet. Before you begin any weight reduction program with your Boxer, consult your veterinarian. There are other conditions, such as hypothyroidism, that can cause significant weight gain.

Degenerative Diseases

Along with old age comes a variety of diseases. Arthritis is common among aging Boxers and can have numerous causes. The end result, however, is a dog with swollen and painful joints. There are many traditional and holistic treatments for arthritis that can result in moderate to excellent pain reduction in your dog. Be sure to consult with your veterinarian for methods of treating this disease.

Eye ulcers (see "corneal ulcers," page 163) are another disease of aging Boxers that tends to strike female, spayed Boxers over the age of five. There are emerging methods for treating this disease if it is caught early enough.

Cancers are serious and this is the age group that is most often struck. Make it a regular part of your routine to brush your Boxer every day and rub your hands over the dog's entire body. *Any* lump or bump should be taken seriously and requires an immediate visit to your veterinarian.

Gingivival hyperplasia is a disease in which a dog's gums grow over its teeth. Geriatric Boxers suffer from this disease; therefore, it is critical that you brush your silver Boxer's teeth routinely—every day if possible—to prevent infections, abscesses, and just plain bad breath.

Cognitive Dysfunction Syndrome

Elderly dogs who become disoriented, experience a significant change in social behaviors (e.g., a friendly Boxer is suddenly afraid of a neighbor he's known all his life), have difficulties sleeping at night, and/or appear confused about the whole concept of housetraining (when no disease is present), are likely suffering from cognitive dysfunction syndrome (CDS), or the loss of cognitive functioning. In more basic terms, it appears as if the dog is going senile.

To some extent, this is exactly what is happening. One CDS study found that 18 percent of dog owners with canines seven years or older reported that their dogs exhibited at least one of the clinical signs of CDS. With dogs aged 11 years and older, 28 percent of owners noticed at least one symptom of CDS, with many owners relating that they saw multiple disease signs.

What does this mean to the Boxer owner? It is quite possible that if you are lucky enough to have a Boxer live past seven years of age, that your aging dog may develop CDS. There are ways to potentially slow the progression of this syndrome through the following:

• Diet—check with your veterinarian for therapeutic foods developed specifically for treating CDS.

• Prescription medications— ANYPRYL (Seleqiline hydrochloride, L-deprenyl) has been shown to temporarily reverse and improve typical CDS behaviors seen in dogs within 30 days.

• Mental stimulation—stimulating the Boxer's senses is thought to help maintain a dog's cognitive function. Taking your Boxer for daily walks where he is allowed to scent, touch, hear, and see new things every day is a good way to keep his mind working. Playing with interactive toys (where the Boxer has to roll, push, or tug something to release a treat), light obedience training, or teaching new, fun tricks to your Boxer are other ways to keep that gray matter working.

Incontinence

This is a topic that is taboo in human conversation and isn't really a hot topic among dog owners either, *but it does happen to many older dogs*, in particular, spayed females. The first issue to be settled when you notice your dog having accidents is that the problem is incontinence and isn't something else, such as a bladder infection or some other illness.

If the incontinence stems from something that is not curable or treatable with medications developed to control this problem, the owner need only show some compassion and creativity to make the Boxer's life continue to be pleasant. One way to help your Boxer with her incontinence is to very closely monitor her eating and drinking and develop a schedule. As with a puppy, if you give your adult enough opportunities to relieve herself throughout her waking hours, she will have less opportunity to have an accident.

Another option you might consider is installing a dog door so the dog can go in and out at will to relieve herself. If the dog simply doesn't realize she has to go until she has gone (while she is sleeping at night, for example) consider purchasing a special bed for incontinent dogs. The pad is made of a fabric that wicks moisture away from the dog. Other beds are constructed with a mesh tray so that the dog can sleep on the tray and allow liquids to drain away from it.

When to Let Go

Unless your aging Boxer passes away quietly in his sleep, you will most likely be faced with a decision that only you can make: Is your dog so ill that he should be euthanized?

The answer to this question should lie exclusively in your dog. In terminal cases, a dog should never have to suffer. If the dog's pain is tolerable—by his standards, not yours—then there's no reason to worry about euthanasia at this point. If, however, the dog is in chronic pain and there is no cure, you need to put aside your feelings as best you can and consider your dog's situation. If there ever was a dog who could understand and even thank you for removing it from its suffering, it is the Boxer. Discuss the problem with your veterinarian.

No one knows the future of any Boxer and an owner can only hope that his or her Boxer will live a full and healthy life. Given the unknowns in life, it is best never to take any Boxer for granted. Learn to treasure every day you are blessed with owning such a very special dog.

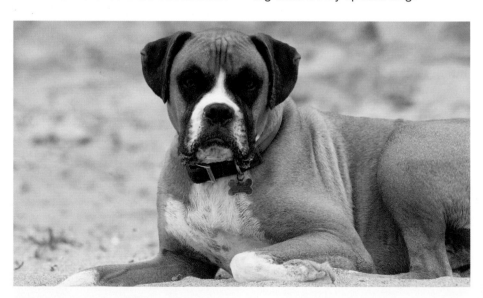

Chapter Eight

Welcome Home!

Welcoming Puppies

Typically, most puppies are brought home at the age of eight weeks or so. The minute you pick up your Boxer puppy, you have taken on a serious responsibility. Separated from his mother, littermates, and the breeder, the puppy is completely dependent on you. You are now the puppy's mother, teacher, and human partner. He cannot survive or thrive without your help.

Fortunately, Boxers are very forgiving of their owners' mistakes, but for the welfare of your Boxer, it's helpful to understand how to care for your puppy, and to understand what those first few days and weeks home will be like.

The First Day

If you've done your homework, your Boxer is coming from a reputable breeder who is scrupulous about breeding for health, conformation, and temperament. Your Boxer puppy is up to date on his vaccinations, he has been wormed appropriately, and his coat is clean and free of fleas and ticks. He is all ready to go home.

Did you remember to make an appointment with your veterinarian? As mentioned earlier in this book, the best plan of action is to drive from the breeder's home to the veterinarian's office for both health and temperament evaluations. If this isn't possible—perhaps you're traveling a long distance or it's a Sunday—make sure you get your puppy in to see your veterinarian as soon as possible, within three days *at the most*. If your puppy appears to be ill before your scheduled appointment, don't hesitate to call your veterinarian, or, if it's after hours when you notice something is wrong, go to the emergency veterinary clinic in your area. Sick puppies can deteriorate rapidly, turning from a little sick to deathly ill in a matter of a day or less. Don't chance it. Get any illness checked out.

When you pick up your puppy he will be fully weaned from his mother. Just because the puppy does not depend on Mom for his meals, however, doesn't mean that he doesn't still depend on her in other ways. Your Boxer puppy will miss his mother the minute you walk out the breeder's door. The puppy will also miss his littermates that have been his constant playmates for the past several weeks or months. For the most part, until you walked into the picture, the Boxer puppy's mother and his littermates were this puppy's entire world. That tumbling mass of Boxer puppies are the canines whom your puppy ate with, played with, and slept with to keep warm. Now all your puppy has is you.

Making the First Night Easier

No matter how great a Boxer owner you are or are going to be, you aren't going to be a suitable replacement for your puppy's mother and littermates—at first. With some exceptions, you can expect the typical Boxer puppy to cry, whimper, bark, and even howl a bit the first

few days—especially when he is left alone.

However, there are things you can do to help gain a little sleep those first few nights and help your puppy make the transformation to his home life a little quicker.

1. Make the puppy feel at home with something that smells familiar. Your young puppy has a very strong sense of smell, and certain scents are very comforting to him. Several days before you go to pick up your puppy, give the breeder a towel or cuddly dog toy and ask if he or she would "scent" the article for you. It takes only a short time of lying on the item by the puppy's mother to embed her scent into the item. Then, when you pick up your puppy to bring him home, you can take this scented item home, too. Having the mother's scent close to the puppy can be extremely comforting and can make for a quieter first few nights.

2. Use a little Dog Appeasing Pheromone (D.A.P.). This compound simulates the hormone that lactating dogs emit when nursing their puppies. Boxer puppies will find this scent very calming. D.A.P. can be sprayed in the crate or on the pup's bedding.

3. Keep the puppy warm. Your Boxer puppy is used to sleeping in a nice, toasty warm puppy pile with all his brothers and sisters. His first night at home may be the first time he sleeps alone—and he could cry simply because he is cold! To keep him warm (without overheating him), fill the bottom third of his crate with shredded newspapers so he can make a deep bed in them. Make sure the crate is in an area free of drafts, and if the room is cold, wrap the sides of the crate (leaving the door unwrapped) with a blanket. You may also wrap a warm hot water bottle in a blanket (if the pup doesn't chew fabric) and place this in the crate, too.

4. Provide a little night music. Studies have shown that some types of music, in particular classical music that is soothing to the ear, are calming to puppies. Avoid pop tunes, rock, and heavy metal.

5. Give him a safe activity. Just as babies often fall asleep while sucking on a bottle or pacifier, many puppies need a good chew toy to help them relax and drift to

Turning to You

When your puppy was with his mother, he turned to her for guidance. If a loud noise startled him, he looked toward his mother to see what her reaction was. If his mother remained calm and unruffled, the puppy realized that the sound of the back door shutting was not scary. If several children ran through the kitchen giggling and laughing and his mother reacted in a gentle, friendly manner, the pup learned that noisy kids are okay.

When you bring your puppy home, he will look to you for guidance. How you react the first time he turns around to see your reaction will mold your future relationship and how he responds to the sights and sounds in his new environment. The best advice is to maintain a confident, friendly posture and an attitude of "it's no big deal." If your Boxer is frightened, don't coddle him and try to physically comfort him: this is telling your puppy that he was right to be frightened and only serves to ingrain in his memory that he *should* respond in a frightened manner. Go about your business as if nothing has happened and your Boxer will adopt your confident attitude over time.

Reward him for friendly, confident, and curious responses to new stimuli; ignore fearful or reactive responses.

sleep. Kong toys with a little peanut butter stuffed inside may be just the noshing trick.

6. Stay close by the little one. In the past, it was thought that babies and puppies should cry themselves to sleep and the parent should not intervene. We now know this creates unnecessary anxiety in a human child, and the same is believed to be true with the puppy. He's always had other dogs and pups with him and now he is alone. That's scary! You're his new "mom," so don't isolate him in a far away room. Put his crate near your bed where he can see, hear, and smell you. Comfort him by stroking him and talking to him. Many owners spend the first few nights on the floor next to their pups' crates so the Boxers know exactly where their owners are.

7. Choose the right type of crate to house your puppy (see page 82). Many Boxers prefer the hard-shell, "denlike" crate. The reason for this is that some dogs feel vulnerable in a wire crate because it is so open. Wrapping a wire crate in a heavy blanket to give it that "den" quality may help; however, your puppy may also discover what fun it is to pull the blanket into the crate to eat, too.

In the excitement of bringing home your puppy, be sure to allow the Boxer to sleep. Little puppies play hard and they need to sleep hard, too. Feed your young charge on a regular schedule (see Nutrition, pages 133–137), and be sure that he does not have to compete for food with other family pets. Also, limit your puppy's exposure to unknown dogs. If you're not sure of the dog's vaccination history, it is better to limit your puppy's exposure until he is fully vaccinated.

Friendship Is a Treat Away

A good way to introduce your puppy to new people is to put him in a *sit* (see page 170). Hand the "stranger" a small bit of treat, and ask him or her to feed it to your puppy. Your puppy will quickly realize that if he is good and sits nicely, he will be richly rewarded. Your neighbors will appreciate the dedication with which you are training your Boxer and will be much more receptive to you and your dog when your puppy reaches his full size. As Boxer owners know, these dogs are pretty much big marshmallows at heart; however, most onlookers are extremely intimidated by the Boxer's strength and powerful bite. Having introduced your puppy in his lovable stage and reinforcing this friendly behavior with treats goes a long way toward establishing good neighbor relations.

The Following Week

After the first week you will begin to notice that life with your Boxer puppy is beginning to get more predictable, if not easier. Don't expect miracles in the house-training department, but your puppy may begin to "hold it" for six hours or so during the night, or at least alert you when he needs to relieve himself.

This is the time period—after the dust has settled from the puppy's first week—when the owner can now begin taking more time to meet the puppy's developmental needs. As previously discussed, this is a critical period for your puppy's socialization. This is when you begin introducing your Boxer puppy to everyone and everything in a controlled manner. You want the people your Boxer meets to be friendly and gentle. You want the dogs he meets to be friendly and gentle, too, and fully vaccinated. And finally, you want the sights and sounds of your neighborhood to be introduced to your puppy in a positive and reinforcing manner. In other words, if a fire engine roars down your street, allow your puppy to be interested, but don't drag him to the street corner to get a better look. Let your puppy take little steps forward and always keep his training positive and consistent.

The Months Ahead

Speaking of training, from the moment your puppy enters your home you should be involved in training him. Whether you realize it or not, everything you do or say around your puppy is part of your puppy's training. For this reason, it is wise to really read up on teaching young puppies so that you won't inadvertently teach your puppy the wrong behaviors. In other words, when your puppy smells dinner being set on the table and he runs over, tries to jump on the chair, and starts barking, what he learns at this point is entirely

dependent on your reaction. Do you look lovingly at the puppy and say, "Oh you cute, sweet thing, here's a little treat for you," thereby encouraging future behavior when the dog is 60 lbs. (27 kg) and capable of jumping on the table and stealing your entire meal, or do you gently pull your puppy from the chair, remove him from the dinner situation, and then put him in a *sit-stay*—rewarding this final behavior with a doggie treat?

Though the example above seems very obvious when written down in black and white, it's not so clear-cut in our day-to-day choices with puppies. Puppies are very cute when they jump up and try to lick us in friendly greetings, but is this the behavior you want your full-grown Boxer to have when your frail Aunt Myrna comes to visit? What about barking? Puppies can be very vocal, but do you want to encourage this behavior in the adult? One owner thought he was so cute when her puppy was growling and barking at the other puppies. Wrong! Dog-dog aggression is not cute and should never be encouraged. But when the owner's response to this aggression was positive, the unwanted behavior was reinforced.

So, as a new owner, be sure to consider how you respond to your Boxer puppy's behaviors. In these first few months, every action counts—and it is often much harder (if not impossible) to "undo" a dog's behavior than it is to prevent the incident from ever occurring in the first place.

Avoiding Bad Experiences

When developing a people-friendly, sociable Boxer, the *quality* of each meeting with a person is far more important than the *quantity* of meetings. Each positive meeting that your Boxer has with a person will build his confidence, and therefore the chances for continued positive introductions. One *bad* or negative meeting (a situation in which the Boxer is frightened) greatly increases the potential for future meetings with strangers to build on the Boxer's fears.

To keep every meeting positive and to build the social, outgoing Boxer you want as a companion and/or family dog, you must understand your pup's body language, and know what steps to take to prevent any fearfulness from entering the meet and greet equation. It may sound difficult, but it just requires an observant owner—one who knows what to do before the Boxer becomes frightened.

In order to prevent a Boxer from becoming frightened, the owner must know the body language for the happy Boxer, the fearful Boxer, and the transitioning Boxer.

The happy, friendly body language of a Boxer is unmistakable: the body has the appearance of being loose, relaxed, and flexible; eyes are soft; tail may be wagging softly or vigorously causing the entire body to "wag"; Boxer may play "bow" (dip low on elbows with rear end up in the air), if exercising; and the mouth is open and panting easily.

Signs of a fearful Boxer are also easy to recognize: head and body may be slightly lower, giving the appearance of cringing or looking upward; pupils dilate (even when it's bright outside), or the pup moves his eyes but not his head, showing the whites of his eyes; aversion of eyes (the pup won't make eye contact); panting becomes nervous (not relaxed); tail may tuck; body may become tense or tremble; pup may flop on his back in a submissive posture; piloerection may occur (raising of hair along back); and pup may try to hide, run away, or start barking or lunging to put more space between himself and the stranger.

If your Boxer puppy is showing signs of fear, he is already having a negative experience. If this happens, take him out of the situation immediately! Never try to force him to meet someone under these circumstances. Do not coddle him and tell him it's okay to meet the person; he will misinterpret your tone of voice as praise for being afraid. Instead, physically remove him from the meeting (confidently and calmly). When you have taken him far enough away from the stranger that the pup can relax and his happy, friendly body language returns, allow him to remain at this distance and simply observe. *Now* you can reward him for being a good boy with praise and a treat.

Recognizing Transition Body Language

The only way to avoid a negative experience is to be able to recognize

when your Boxer is transitioning from a relaxed state to a stressed state, and remove him from the situation. The transitioning is relatively easy to spot *if you know what body language signs to look for in your puppy*. Basically, it's the *lack* of friendly, relaxed behavior. The moment your Boxer begins to tense his body, raise or lower his head position (either becoming aggressive or frightened), stop wagging his tail or start tensing at the base of his tail, starts panting (when he wasn't before) or stops panting (when he was previously panting), you need to back him out of the situation. Calmly take him to a distance at which he can observe comfortably. This may be five feet away or across the street. Once you've got him comfortable, reward him for his good behavior. Work on gradually decreasing the distance over time.

Learning your lifestyle: For the first month your puppy is home, it is also important to introduce him to your lifestyle. You'll want to take the puppy on frequent rides in the car. If you are using a crate in your home, make sure your puppy is comfortable with his new home. Do the garbage trucks come on Thursday mornings? Make sure your Boxer is able to see the trucks and is rewarded for good behavior. Steps in the house, toilets flushing, and vacuum cleaners running are other situations that you will want your Boxer to be comfortable with and not to fear.

To reinforce positive reactions to these "stimuli," catch the puppy when he responds appropriately, without fear or aggression, and reward that behavior with a treat. Watch your puppy carefully when on walks for transitioning behaviors. Just as you don't want any negative reactions when socializing with people, you want all your Boxer's experiences in his environment (in and out of the house) to be as positive as possible, too. If your Boxer spots something in the home that he's not sure about but wants to investigate, allow him to make his own approach. A dog who is allowed to make his own approach is most likely to have a positive experience. If, however, your Boxer is approaching something that is going to make a sudden scary noise or that you know might injure him, intervene and take him out of the situation.

When on walks—and the pup is on leash—the Boxer is not allowed to make his own approach. He is tethered to you, so it is critical that you pay attention to his body language. If something is causing him unease or stress (perhaps the approach of a large garbage truck), move him farther away from the object until he is able to observe the object from what he feels is a safe distance. Reward happy, confident body language; ignore other behaviors.

Remember, too, that the quality of the experiences is the most important aspect when introducing your puppy to both people and his environment. One bad experience can make a lifelong impression. Multiple good experiences can shape a confident, outgoing Boxer as an adult. So keep his experiences positive. Reward for good behavior. Your efforts will be rewarded tenfold in the future with a well-adjusted, social Boxer.

Welcoming the Rescued Boxer

Some rescued Boxers walk into a home, take a look around, and settle in as if they have lived there all their lives. They're house-trained, have nice manners, and know several helpful commands. Sound like a dream? OK, in many instances it is. Remember the primary reason dogs are given up to shelters? *They are not trained.* They are good dogs who have been allowed to behave badly.

The problems of rescued Boxers, however, are rarely insurmountable. If they were, a responsible rescue would not be placing the dog. And, for a person with prior Boxer experience, transitioning an adult Boxer into a new home may seem quite simple. For the inexperienced Boxer owner, there are a few "adopted" dog tips you should consider.

The First Day

Bringing home an adopted Boxer can be every bit as exciting as bringing home a new puppy. It can also be just as exhausting. Here are a few ideas as to what you can expect and how you can make this day less stressful.

1. First, before you leave to pick up your adopted Boxer, have your home ready. Read through the chapter Preparing for the New Arrival, page 77, and prepare yourself well. With a puppy, you may have a couple of days' grace period before the real destruction kicks in. With an adult dog, there is no grace period. If you don't want your dog in carpeted areas at first—a good idea—then make these areas inaccessible. If your gate to the backyard doesn't shut all the way, fix it now. And, be sure to purchase a sturdy dog crate that will fit your new Boxer. Your adoption agency should be able to give you an exact size based on the dog's height and length.

2. When you go to pick up your Boxer, take the crate in your car. When transporting your Boxer home from the rescue or adoption facility, you should use a crate. There are several reasons for this. The first is that you do not know this dog yet. If he panics when a motorcycle guns past your car, you could end up with a full-grown Boxer trying to crawl into your lap while you barrel down the highway at 65 miles (105 km) per hour. It is safer for both you and your new dog if your dog rides in either a travel crate or a partitioned section of your vehicle.

The second reason for restraining—we won't say "caging"—your Boxer during his first ride with you is that this literally could be one of his *very first* car rides. A nervous Boxer may drool profusely, shake, pace, throw up, or relieve himself. Also, a shelter Boxer may be infested with fleas or ticks or be suffering from a parasitic infection (worms, giardia). If the dog is crated, the damage is minimal. If the dog is loose, well, at a minimum you'll have a mess. If the dog is suffering from something more serious, you may suffer more serious consequences, too.

3. Next, make sure you take your Boxer directly to your veterinarian for a complete health and temperament evaluation. If you adopted your Boxer from a breed rescue, these services may have already been performed. If your Boxer tested negative on his heartworm test and is on preventive medicine, fine, you don't need to have this tested again. Likewise, if the dog has verification of all his vaccinations, there's no need to repeat these. However, have your veterinarian evaluate your Boxer's temperament. Though the Boxer is renowned and treasured for his even, loving temperament, and has been known to endure past lives in abusive situations and still maintain this inherent temperament, it is always a wise move to have the dog evaluated carefully. This evaluation is particularly important if you are adopting the Boxer from a facility that does not offer this service. It is equally wise to have your veterinarian evaluate your Boxer, even when you have adopted him from a reputable breed rescue or a breeder. A second opinion can be invaluable.

The veterinarian may just pick up on some quirk that eluded the foster "parents" of the dog. Do it.

4. If your dog is coming from a shelter and has not been bathed, groomed, or dipped, make sure your next appointment is with the groomer. This has been mentioned previously in this book, but it really bears repeating: Don't bring home a dirty, infested dog. Why subject your other pets or yourself to something you don't have to? The grooming fee for bathing, dipping (if necessary), and drying a Boxer is not substantial and it will make your first day a bit easier. The only exception to this suggestion is a case in which the nerves of the adopted Boxer may not quite be up to the hustle and bustle of the grooming shop. If this describes your Boxer, you may have to be a little more careful and enlist the help and expertise of a more experienced Boxer owner.

5. Once your adult Boxer is home, you'll want to walk him right away upon exiting the car. Resist the temptation to immediately bring him into your home or parade him past the neighbors. There'll be plenty of time for that later. To help begin house-training, or to reinforce the training the Boxer already has, try to have him relieve himself in his new yard.

6. Once your Boxer has done his outdoor duties, then you can bring your new dog into the home. Again, resist taking your Boxer places he won't be allowed to go initially. Keep the Boxer in his area. Show him where his bed or crate will be. Give him some fresh cool water. Bring out a few interesting dog toys and a safe chew bone. Speak gently with your new adult and offer him a few hand-held treats. Your Boxer will be very curious and you can expect him to check out his area and you quite thoroughly.

How long it takes for your dog to begin showing signs of relaxing in your home really depends on the individual dog. Some rescued adults walk into a house, find the softest place they're allowed to lie on, and crash from their hectic first day. Others may trot around the house and yard for an hour or more. Be sure to allow your Boxer to relieve himself frequently—either by walks or in the yard—to avoid any nervous mistakes in your home. To avoid a potential bout with bloat (see pages 153–154), make sure your Boxer has settled down comfortably before you feed him a meal. If your Boxer is uneasy throughout the day, you may want to hand-feed him bits of food at a time rather than one large meal.

Recognize Signs of Stress

Until your Boxer has bonded with you, which may take several days to several weeks, understand that a

Other Signs of Stress
- Dilated pupils
- Blinking
- Tightening of eye lids
- Avoiding eye contact
- Ears spreading sideways or laying back on neck
- Lip licking
- Yawning
- Shaking (as if shaking off water but not wet)
- Rapid changes in rate of tail wagging (fast to slow, raised to lowered)
- Overall body signs of uncertainty

dog who is under stress may react to stimuli in ways he would never react once he's comfortable in his new home. Allow the dog to investigate at his own pace. Do not invite neighbors, the kids' friends, and relatives over to meet the new dog; you'll overwhelm him. Remember, you want all of his new experiences with you to be positive. Spend the first week with your new Boxer in the quiet of your home and on walks around the neighborhood without the entire block converging on the new dog.

Know the signs of stress, too (see page 115), and follow your adult Boxer's lead when meeting people outdoors. Follow the same guidelines as you would with a puppy's socialization (see page 114), rewarding only good behaviors and avoiding any negative experiences.

The First Night

When it comes time to settle down for the night, walk your Boxer one more time, allowing him to relieve himself. Then, put him in his crate, which should be lined with a thick layer of shredded newspaper. (When you've had your Boxer for a while, and he's not under as much stress, you can try lining his crate with soft blankets, old towels, or a nice crate pad. Even then, watch him carefully to make sure he doesn't chew or suck on his towels. Even a small piece of fabric can present a choking hazard or cause the Boxer to become impacted.) Then brace yourself. If you thought a puppy was noisy when left alone his first night, you'll be impressed with the sounds and noises that can come from an adult Boxer. The adult Boxer obviously is not troubled with a puppy's pangs of leaving his littermates and mother; however, he could be uncomfortable with a change in lifestyle, even though this new lifestyle is in most cases significantly better than what he was used to.

In basic terms, some adopted dogs simply handle change better than others. On the first night in a new home, some adult Boxers will put their heads down and immediately go to sleep in the comfort and safety of their crate, seemingly appreciative of everything you've done for them. Other adult Boxers are less than thrilled with a different routine and are more likely to vocalize on their uncertainty.

What do you do? You can put a particularly attractive chew toy or bone in the Boxer's crate to help keep his mind off the separation. You can also stroke and talk to the Boxer to reassure him. Put the Boxer's crate where he can see you sleep.

For the most part, the adult Boxer will adjust very quickly to his new surroundings and will not keep his new owners awake for very many nights. Since he has excellent control over his bodily functions, he also will be able to sleep through the night—assuming he is fed on a schedule that permits this.

Getting to Know Each Other

Often, the only information that a rescue or adoption facility has on a Boxer is what the staff has observed while the Boxer has been in its care. Little is known about the Boxer's past. Was he socialized with other pets? Is he tolerant of children? Will he jump fences or dig holes? Is he terrorized by thunder? Does he have any phobias?

The first month or two of owning an adopted Boxer is a learning period for both dog and human. During this time, your Boxer very well may behave like a big puppy, investigating every aspect of your home with wonder and true Boxer amazement. A flushing toilet may invoke a playful response. In some instances, the same stimulus may evoke an apprehensive or even fearful response in a less confident dog. Your Boxer may never have seen a

screen before and might charge through your door, ripping down and shredding a lightweight screen door. Glass windows may not be recognized as being solid; be sure to introduce your Boxer to the windows just to make sure this isn't the case.

If your Boxer was mistreated, it will also be a time for him to learn to trust humans again. Kindness, patience, and love work wonders. Sometimes you may discover that something in your home elicits a fearful response from your Boxer. You will need to work toward conditioning your dog to overcome his fears. Generally, this involves ignoring fearful responses and rewarding positive behaviors. While in the house and acclimating to the sounds and routine of daily living, your Boxer will be able to make his own approach to scary things. Often, this is all that it takes for him to overcome any trepidation he might have regarding unique sounds, objects, and other inanimate things in your home. If, however, your adopted Boxer is nervous or stressed around a family member, it is best to consult with a good trainer for tips tailored to *your*

Boxer and your family's situation to help ease the tension and make sure everyone is the best of friends. (Tip: Behavior modification training may not be limited to the Boxer; the family member may be doing something that is frightening the Boxer.)

Training

Even if your Boxer comes to you well trained or trained enough to navigate effectively through day-to-day living, you still need to take him through basic obedience. Training your dog and working on commands on a daily basis will help establish a strong bond between you and your dog. It also helps to enforce who is the leader in the relationship. Of course, another major benefit to taking your dog to training classes is that you have a wonderful contact for advice on problems. An experienced and reputable trainer is a real treasure to know. Cultivate this contact and do not hesitate to consult with your trainer for any behavioral dilemmas. You also can always contact your breed rescue person for advice and tips.

Above all, with an adopted Boxer the rule is to *take things slowly.* Do not expect too much from your adopted Boxer too soon. Remember, whether they are baby steps or giant leaps, any progress in the right direction is still progress. Most adult Boxers will adjust quickly to their new homes, but it's far better to make this adjustment safely and lovingly than to rush a dog. Your newly adopted Boxer will gladly give you his entire life to share if you just take the time to ease him into your life. You'll be glad you took the time.

The Rescued Boxer as a Second Dog

Owning Boxers can become addictive and sometimes just one Boxer isn't enough. (Two Boxers can have such great fun together!) Many times, Boxer owners choose to rescue an adult Boxer as their second dog. To add a second dog to the family, both the dog selection and the initial introduction of the two dogs is critical to making the relationship work. As mentioned before, if a Boxer holds a grudge against another Boxer, the two may have to be separated for life. If you've ever had to try to separate two vibrant, strong, and determined Boxers from "getting at each other" for the rest of their lives, you know this is not a situation to be taken lightly and requires serious commitment by all who live in the house. Trying to separate two Boxers who are engaged in a fight to the death is very, very dangerous and virtually ensures that those who try to separate the dogs will receive several deep bite wounds themselves. Prevention is the best protection against a grudge match evolving between two otherwise completely loving and sweet dogs.

Dog Selection

When considering a second Boxer for your family, it is important to try to find a match that will cause the least amount of friction. Male-female pairings generally work best. If you have an adult male in the home, for example, choosing an adult female as the second dog will maximize your chances of the two getting along, or at least tolerating each other.

Same-sex pairings can be successful, too, but great care needs to be given in determining the overall compatibility of the two dogs, with special attention given in determining the dominance level of each dog. A same-sex pairing would not be recommended for new Boxer owners unless they are working with an experienced Boxer rescue that spends time and effort in evaluating not only the dog in their possession (and in need of adoption), but also the resident dog of the potential adopters.

The reason same-sex pairings among Boxers can be trickier is that there is always a shakedown period in which the two dogs determine who is boss and who is second in command. The same head butting does not seem to occur nearly as often when the two dogs are of the opposite sex. Typically, the resident dog retains his status as top dog and the new dog takes her place as subordinate. When the new dog is young, strong, and virile (with males) or young, strong, and dominant (females), the younger dog will often challenge the authority or ranking of the resident dog. Few Boxers are willing to give up this position of power, and then same-sex problems occur. Once a squabble occurs, it rarely is settled. Future arguments ensue, with the level of the fights escalating into a horrible and even deadly mess.

To avoid the first squabble from occurring, it is important that the new dog is introduced properly to the resident dog. Even after the dogs seem to be getting along well, it is always advisable to keep the adult dogs separated and in crates while the owner is out of the home.

The Introduction

Much of how the resident Boxer will take to the new Boxer (and vice versa) depends on how they are introduced. The Boxer rescue you adopted your dog from will be able to give you additional advice on helping dogs accept each other. In some cases, the rescue may suggest replacing the rescued Boxer with one that is less confrontational. Just as some people don't get along well with other people, some Boxers may require a single-dog home, but these dogs are generally the exception rather than the rule. Most Boxers, if paired well and introduced in a safe and calm manner, welcome the addition of another playmate.

• **Introduce the dogs on neutral territory.** Have a family member bring the resident Boxer to a park or grassy area where you have the new Boxer. Do not ask the dogs to meet and greet each other; instead, walk side-by-side with your family member. Your goal is for the Boxers to walk peacefully with a little distance between them.

• **Introduce the dogs off-leash on neutral territory.** If the walking went well, try introducing the two at an empty neutral dog park. With one Boxer in the play area and the other Boxer *off-leash* in the holding area, the two Boxers can meet and greet and sniff each other through the fence. You should be able to tell if the two are showing positive, friendly behaviors. If there are any signs of stress, or if one or the other Boxer acts aggressively, separate the two dogs. If all goes well, allow the dog in the holding area to join in play in the larger area. Keep moving throughout the park so that the dogs keep moving, too. Watch for any play that might go over the top and call out the resident dog before either dog gets offended.

• **Keep the dogs separate at home.** Allow the Boxers to see each other through pet gates or alternating who is in the crate. There should be no signs of stress displayed by either dog, nor should there be any signs of aggression or fear. If one of the Boxers appears to be showing less-than-friendly body language, physically separate the dogs so that they are not near each other.

• **Shower the resident dog with lots of great things.** Usually, the attention in the house is given to the new dog. Don't do this! Take your resident dog for more walks, give him more toys, feed him more meals (break his daily ration into more meals so he thinks he's getting more meals), teach him new tricks, work on obedience skills, and take him on car rides. All this attention helps to make the resident dog connect great things with the arrival of the new dog.

• **Continue side-by-side walks.** Don't rush into letting the new dog have all the rights and privileges of the resident dog. Depending on how well the two dogs ignore each other on walks, you can begin allowing them to play for short periods together in the yard. Watch carefully and end the play when both dogs are still having fun. Continue to keep the dogs separated with gates (and in crates when you're gone) for the majority of the day and night.

• **Gradually allow more free play together.** Over a period of weeks, allow the dogs more playtime together. If you see any stressful behavior being displayed by either Boxer, calmly separate the two and give them time to settle down.

• **Help maintain the resident Boxer's status.** You can help to do this by feeding him first, and giving him attention first. You are the ultimate leader of your dogs, and most dogs should recognize your authority and which dog you recognize as the leader of the dog pack.

Chapter Nine
Grooming and Feeding

Boxers are a joy to care for in the grooming and feeding department. After the initial time and expense that may be incurred if you choose to have a puppy's ears cropped, the Boxer is truly a low-maintenance breed. This is not to say, however, that the Boxer is a no-maintenance dog. If you want your canine to sport a glossy coat, have a sparkle in his eyes, and have physical strength and energy, you'll need to invest some effort in your Boxer's upkeep.

Brushing

Beginning with the basics, brushing a shorthaired breed such as the Boxer is relatively simple; perhaps *remembering* to brush your pet from time to time is actually the hard part. If you don't brush your Boxer's coat on a regular basis, he will shed. It's part of the natural process of being a dog. Old hair falls out; new hair grows in. The only bad part is that white hairs invariably fall on dark-colored upholstery and clothes, and dark hairs lodge themselves deeply into the only white chair in the house!

As for brushing, your Boxer will enjoy a daily brushing with a brush—soft natural or rubber bristles that will catch the hairs are fine—but once a week should suffice to keep too many hairs from dropping into your furniture and on your floors.

Spring shedding is not a problem with this breed because the Boxer rarely has a winter coat to shed. For the most part, Boxers do not fare well in cold weather and much prefer the warmth of their human companion's home and hearth to the elements of the outside. Therefore, a well-kept Boxer will never develop any winter thickness to his coat because he simply isn't outside for any period of time. However, don't take this to mean that a Boxer could be kept outside and he would develop a thick coat. A thicker coat, perhaps, but nothing substantial enough to keep him warm in cold weather.

Brush Puppies Early
To make grooming a pleasurable experience for all, it is wise to begin brushing your puppy on a daily basis. Though your puppy may not need brushing this frequently, it is

generally easier to get a small puppy to stand still for grooming than it is an older puppy who is untamed to the ways of the brush.

A good time to brush your puppy is after he has played hard and is almost ready to sleep. With the puppy relaxed and in your lap, you can gently begin stroking him. Older puppies can be put in a *stand-stay* and brushed in this manner. If you are planning on showing your Boxer, you will want to accustom him to a grooming table when he is young, too.

With puppies of any age, gently discourage any chewing of the brush; otherwise, when your Boxer is larger, you'll find yourself on the losing end of a tug-of-war battle.

Bathing

Unless your Boxer makes it a habit to tunnel through your flower beds on a regular basis, you really won't have to bathe him very often. Weekly brushing should be enough to keep your dog's skin healthy and to keep the shedding of hairs at a minimum. Bathing your Boxer is really only necessary when he has particularly dirtied himself or if he begins to smell a bit too doggy.

When bathing your Boxer, consider your puppy or dog's comfort level. Use a tub indoors, and use warm water when wetting and rinsing your Boxer. No dog enjoys icy water, and puppies are particularly sensitive to cold water. Make the

bath enjoyable and healthy for your Boxer and there will be less of a struggle later.

Also, while bathing your dog, try to avoid getting water or soap in his eyes and ears. Soap can burn a dog's eyes. As for your dog's ears, it is important to minimize their contact with water because a dog's ears are constructed differently than a human's and do not naturally drain as well.

Tip: If your dog receives frequent baths or enjoys playing in area lakes, streams, or other bodies of water, you may want to invest in a

Bathing Tip

When you do bathe your Boxer, use a shampoo that is formulated specifically for dogs. Human shampoos are designed for a different pH level and will dry a dog's skin. They may also irritate your Boxer's eyes. If your Boxer has dry skin or skin allergies, be sure to consult with your veterinarian about specific shampoos that can be used to help rather than increase this problem.

bottle of a cleansing/ear-drying solution. This helps dry trapped fluid in the Boxer's ear, as well as prevent a bacterial infection or a yeast imbalance.

After your Boxer's bath is completed and you've thoroughly washed all the soap out of the puppy or dog's coat, you can towel-dry your dog. Make sure that your Boxer can finish his drying in a warm, comfortable place; this is not the time for cold drafts. Also, you may want to make sure your Boxer can't run free in the backyard when he is still damp. As soon as you let him out in the yard, he is sure to dig a hole or roll in a muddy patch. It's not that your Boxer is being spiteful; it's just that it feels so good. To keep yourself happy and your Boxer clean, try to keep the dog or puppy restrained until his coat has dried.

Clean It All

When bathing your dog, clean his bedding, too. There's nothing more

disheartening than to have shampooed and washed your Boxer only to have him run over and rub himself all over his smelly old bed. Most beds have removable covers that can be washed. If you've had the inside padding for a while, you may want to replace that, too.

Ears

As mentioned earlier, a dog's ears should not be exposed to water or soap during a bath. So, how do you clean them? Unless your dog is troubled with ear infections, all you need to do is take a clean cotton ball and wipe as much of the ear as possible. *Do not use a cotton swab to reach the dog's ear canal.* This is very dangerous and unnecessary.

Check your dog's ears frequently for odors. An ear infection will have a very foul smell. There may also be a lot of discharge coming from your dog's ear or ears. If either symptom is present in your Boxer's ears, get him to the veterinarian immediately. Untreated outer ear infections can progress quickly into a serious condition.

Cropping

If you've decided you want to have your puppy's ears cropped, the most important thing you must do is work with an experienced and talented ear-cropping veterinarian. It is illegal and extremely dangerous to have a layperson attempt to crop a Boxer's ears. Ear cropping is considered major surgery for a dog and requires that the dog be under general anesthesia for more than an hour. Make absolutely sure that you have this procedure performed by a skilled veterinarian.

Of course, you don't want just any veterinarian cropping ears. There is a true art to cutting the ear into a long show crop; an inexperienced or sloppy cropping job can ruin a Boxer's chances of ever doing well in the show ring. Therefore, seek out a highly qualified veterinarian who is strongly recommended by Boxer breeders in your area.

In addition to simply having a good eye, steady hands, and a knack for working with Boxer ears, the veterinary surgeon must take several factors into consideration when cropping a puppy's ears: the weight of the ear leather—thin ears will stand with higher points than a thicker, heavier ear flap—the shape of the puppy's ear cartilage, and the puppy's muscle control and age.

Postsurgical care: Once the ears are successfully cropped, the complete success of the ear crop now falls on the owner and his or her ability and commitment to carefully follow the veterinarian's postsurgical care instructions. If an owner is not committed to keeping the wounds clean (at least twice daily for four to five days), and visiting his or her veterinarian every two weeks for checking the ears' progress and retapings, an ear cropping can be a terrible mistake. The cut edges can become infected in the early stages and

improper attention to subsequent taping can produce a dog with floppy rather than erect cropped ears. Working with the cropped ears until they are set properly and stand erect can take anywhere from two weeks to six months or more if there are difficulties.

If you are going to invest the time and money in cropped ears, invest it in an experienced, qualified veterinarian and be prepared to commit to months of biweekly visits to your veterinarian for retaping the dog's ears.

Do-it-yourselfers: There are books on the market and websites on the Internet that show detailed methods of posting ears either with mole foam or the more traditional "plug and tape" techniques. Though these outlines are very descriptive and come from reliable, experienced sources, the reality of doing this job yourself is not discussed. Imagine trying to convince a wiggly Boxer puppy that he really does want a cardboard tampon applicator wrapped in sticky tape stuck into each ear. Or, picture attempting to remove mole foam that had been

applied with surgical glue two weeks ago, and then convincing this same puppy that you're going to re-glue fresh mole foam to his ears for another week.

If you are a very experienced breeder, you may have done these procedures scores of times and feel very comfortable performing all of your puppy's postsurgical care yourself. You know the ins and outs, you know how to use olive oil or ointments when massaging the ears, and you know how to correct ears that are pitching inward. If you are new to the breed, however, or just don't want to bother with this by yourself, make sure you budget for the necessary veterinary visits. This is certainly not the time to try to save money. How you care for your Boxer's newly cropped ears in these first few months will affect how your Boxer looks for the remainder of his life.

Nail Care

Trimming your Boxer's toenails should be a regular part of your dog-grooming efforts. Some dogs' nails grow quickly; others seem to remain short for long periods of time. Whether your Boxer's nails grow quickly or slowly, they should always be kept short. Long nails can cause a dog's toes to spread in awkward and uncomfortable positions. They also catch easier and can cause your dog to break a nail or pull the entire nail from the toe—both very painful.

Trimming nails is relatively easy if you begin conditioning your Boxer as a puppy. Wait until the puppy is tired after playing or eating. While he is lying down, gently hold each paw and touch the nail trimmer to the puppy's toenails. Reward the puppy for his good behavior with a treat. Do this on a daily basis. When the puppy's nails have finally grown enough to actually trim—this may be a couple of weeks—you can clip the tips of the nails. Since the puppy is so small at this point, a regular toenail clipper will be too large to accurately clip the nails. Try using a clipper for toy breeds or even a cat's claw trimmer. These smaller nail trimmers are easier to maneuver with little nails. As your Boxer grows, you can purchase a larger nail trimmer.

How to trim: The most important part of clipping a dog's toenails is to avoid cutting into the "quick," or the nail's blood supply. If your Boxer has white paws, he will most likely have clear nails on some, if not all of his toes. With a clear nail, it is very easy to see where the quick ends in the nail. Place the trimmers a smidge beyond the end of the quick, and trim quickly. If your Boxer has some black or dark nails, use the amount you trimmed from the clear nail as a guide for where to place the trimmer on these nails. If your Boxer has all dark nails, you will have to look more closely at the nail to find where the quick ends.

It is always a good idea to keep a towel nearby when trimming, in case you do "quick" the dog. Also, there are products on the market that promptly stop the bleeding of a quicked toenail; you should have some handy when you are trimming nails.

Another way to trim nails is with an electric grinder that grinds the nails to a smooth finish. It takes a little longer than clipping, and it makes more noise. It also vibrates slightly and the ground toenails do smell a bit, but if you get your Boxer used to this procedure, it can be an efficient way to trim nails. Many people use the grinder to smooth out their dog's toenails after they've been clipped.

If you can't clip your Boxer's toenails for some reason, make sure to take your dog to a groomer to have this done on a regular basis. Every month to six weeks should be sufficient, with some Boxers requiring less frequent visits.

Dental Care

Brush a Boxer's teeth? If this suggestion from your veterinarian takes you off guard, consider these recent statistics: Most dogs (85 percent) over the age of four have periodontal disease. They also have bad breath. Back in the old days of dog ownership, not much thought was given to a dog's teeth other than opting to feed dry food rather than moist and perhaps to keep good chew toys or bones available to the dog. The concept of taking a brush to a dog's teeth was totally foreign, except perhaps to exhibitors who worked to make every aspect of the Boxer as presentable as possible.

Of course, back in the old days, a lot of dogs had a lot fewer teeth.

To prevent bad breath, gum disease, tartar buildup, and tooth loss,

the strong recommendation by the veterinary community is to get your puppy accustomed to having his teeth brushed at least one or more times a week. One of the easiest ways to begin this process is to use what is called a finger brush—a soft plastic nubby cylinder that fits over your finger. Your puppy or adult is much less likely to balk at your fingers going in his mouth, especially when covered in a delectable chicken- or beef-flavored canine toothpaste, than he would be if you tried to use a dog toothbrush. The best time to attempt to introduce your Boxer to a tooth brushing is when he is tired and content. With regular practice, you will eventually be able to use a toothbrush.

Toothpaste for Dogs

You may be tempted to pull out your favorite toothpaste and use it on your dog in a pinch, but resist this temptation; the effects could be very detrimental. Toothpaste designed for humans should never be used on a dog's teeth. The ingredients in human products can be harmful to dogs if swallowed. Since it's impossible to teach a Boxer to spit, it's best to use products that are both effective in cleaning the dog's teeth and safe for a dog to swallow.

Other Homecare Foods and Products

There is some evidence that hard kibble foods are better at keeping a dog's teeth clean of plaque than canned food; however, with that said, the Boxer has to actually *chew* his food. Many Boxers eat their dinners chewing nary a morsel of food. They literally swallow the chunks of kibble whole. If your Boxer doesn't chew his food, it won't matter whether you serve him dry food or moist food. If, on the other hand, you have a neater eater who *does* indeed chew his kibbles, then feeding him a dry food can be beneficial.

In addition, the Veterinary Oral Health Council (VOHC) regularly reviews products that purport to assist in preventing the buildup of plaque on dog's teeth. Products that have been reviewed and received the VOHC's seal of approval will have this information printed prominently on the packaging. Products that are reviewed include prescription diets designed specifically to clean dogs' teeth, as well as chews, treats, and antiplaque water additives.

Even with regular home maintenance and specialty foods and chews, the Boxer will still require professional teeth cleaning.

Veterinary Cleaning

Boxers have notoriously bad teeth and require a higher level of care than many other dog breeds. Boxer owners should budget for an annual dental cleaning performed by their veterinarians. This process is not inexpensive and typically costs more than $100, depending on how much work is necessary. A routine veterinary dental cleaning includes: anesthetizing the Boxer;

X-raying the teeth to assess the below-the-gumline health of the dog's teeth; flushing the mouth with an antibacterial solution; removing all calculus above and below the gumline (this can only be done while a dog is anesthetized); polishing the teeth to remove microscopic scratching that may have occurred during scaling; and flushing the mouth with antibacterial solution again.

Nutrition

Proper maintenance of your Boxer requires that you also feed him well. That does not mean to kill your dog with kindness and overfeed him. Feeding your dog well in this context means to meet your dog's nutritional requirements. A properly fed Boxer will have energy and a wonderfully glossy coat. He may also have less opportunity to develop certain diseases and disorders that are related to malnutrition or obesity.

Finding the best food for your Boxer, however, is not necessarily an easy task. One walk down the aisle of any pet store and an owner can quickly get confused about which food to choose. Reading the labels may not help much if you don't know what you're looking for, and just because a food is packaged attractively and is very expensive doesn't mean your Boxer will thrive on it.

What you need to consider is how the food is packaged, what nutrients it includes, and for what life stage it was developed. The following is a brief nutrition primer that will help you make the right choice in selecting your dog's food.

Packaging

There are three basic ways dog foods are packaged: canned, semimoist, or dry. In some areas, you may be able to purchase meat-based products that are frozen or refrigerated.

Canned: Canned foods are mostly water (up to 75 percent or more) and are the most expensive of commercial dog foods. Canned foods generally contain few preservatives because of the processes involved in the canning procedure, but they also contain a high percentage of fat. Because the food is soft, it does not provide your Boxer with any teeth-cleaning benefits.

Semimoist: Semimoist foods are high in sugars, can be expensive, and generally are not recommended for dogs by veterinarians.

Dry: Dry foods may help avoid tooth decay if a Boxer chews his food and doesn't swallow it whole. Dry foods contain the least amount of fat and are economical to feed. On the flip side, dry foods have the greatest amount of preservatives among dog foods, and the dry food does expand in a dog's stomach, which may cause problems in a Boxer who is predisposed to or has a higher risk of developing bloat.

Refrigerated foods: A few pet food manufacturers are now marketing freshly made foods that are kept in the refrigerator section. These foods can be found at grocery stores, pet food stores, and specialty pet stores. They come in large, sausagelike containers or tubs and are dated with a "sell by" date. Once opened, the foods must be used within a certain number of days. If these foods meet minimum feeding requirement recommended by the Association of American Feed Control Officials (AAFCO) (see page 135), they can be used as the Boxer's entire meal or mixed with a kibble. The only drawback to a healthy refrigerated dog food is that it will be substantially more expensive to feed a medium-to-large Boxer than most other foods.

Frozen: Frozen dog foods are not widely available. They often have to be ordered in larger quantities and shipped, which can be cost-prohibitive unless you are sharing your food order with other Boxer owners. These foods are also sometimes available from vendors at dog shows. If you happen to like a frozen dog food, you can find out from the vendor when he or she will be in your area. Purchasing bulk at a show can save on expensive shipping costs. Some frozen foods are also available in some pet stores. Generally considered to be high-quality foods, the main drawback to frozen dog foods is the cost. Storage can be a problem with these foods, but if you're willing to invest in an outdoor garage freezer or forego your personal ice cream stash in the home, this may not be a problem.

Life Stages

In addition to developing several types of dog foods, manufacturers produce foods specifically created to meet the particular nutritional requirements of certain life stages. These life stages may include puppy, adult, and obese adult or senior. Other special feeds are designed for active dogs, and those with specific health problems, such as dental disease, allergies, or diabetes. If your Boxer is younger than 18 months, you will most likely want to go with a quality puppy food. As an adult, your Boxer may not require anything more than a basic, well-balanced adult formula, or he may need a high-performance active dog brand in order to keep enough weight on him. Senior diets are often packaged to attract purchasers who apply human traits to their dogs and believe that their dogs will be happier eating *more* of *less* food, than less of the food they are currently eating. Some senior foods, however, do have different nutritional values and perhaps digestibility factors that may make them specific to this age group. Again, careful label reading will be able to tell you something about these foods.

What Your Boxer Really Needs

Look for a quality food made by a recognized manufacturer that meets your dog's daily nutritional require-ments and is palatable; if it doesn't taste great, it doesn't matter what is in the food—your Boxer won't eat it. The food should show on the label that it has been certified by AAFCO or the Canadian Veterinary Medical Association (CVMA), depending on where you live. AAFCO and CVMA certifications confirm that the food has been assessed in feeding trials for a certain life stage. In other words, instead of simply providing a nutrient analysis, these certified foods have undergone feeding trials to prove that they at least meet minimal standards. It would be nice if there were more refined tests that could gauge the exact standards that are met, but at this time there are no requirements for refined testing.

Homemade Diets

Another option that is available to owners is to prepare fresh meals for your Boxer. Though this method takes time and requires a well-prepared recipe designed by a veterinary nutritionist, it can be done. Owners should be advised that developing fresh meals on a daily basis requires dedication. If your idea of a fresh meal for yourself is popping a frozen dinner in the microwave, opening up a bag of prepackaged lettuce, and pouring on a little bottled dressing, then preparing fresh meals for your Boxer is probably not going to be for you.

If you are willing to try this method, however, it can make a night-and-day difference in the overall health of your dog. You are exposing your dog to few if any preservatives or chemicals. The meals contain fresh meat and vegetables, and supplements tailored to your Boxer's needs. This method is not cheap, nor can any shortcuts be taken. There is not much room for creativity, either. The dog's nutritional requirements need to be met, so don't go substituting or swapping ingredients on a whim. Follow your veterinarian's recipe and make only those changes he or she has approved or requested.

Looking for Variety?

A great source for multiple diets that are all nutritionally balanced and developed by a veterinary nutritionist can be found at *www. BalanceIt.com*. When on the website, you select the protein your dog likes (e.g., skinless roasted chicken, baked Atlantic salmon, pan-browned ground beef), and a carbohydrate (e.g., cooked long-grain rice, cooked oats, cooked sweet potato without the skin, cooked enriched spaghetti, etc.). A list of recipes is then provided to you with additional vegetables, oils, foods, and supplements. There is a fee for each recipe selected, but you

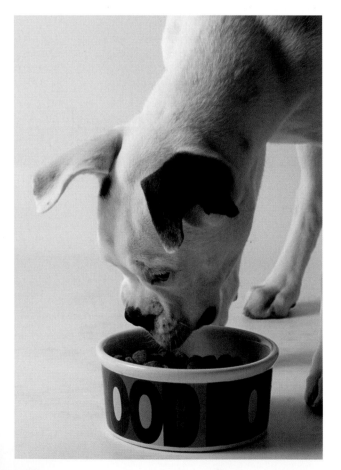

can choose whether to purchase the supplements from the drugstore (supplements packaged for humans) or Balance IT canine supplements available through the website.

When to Feed

Young puppies should have their feeding spaced so that they can eat three times a day. Once your Boxer is a year old, he can be fed twice a day. Though some owners choose for convenience to feed their dogs once a day, this is not wise, as feeding one large meal can greatly increase the risk that your Boxer may suffer from bloat (see page 153 for more information). It is healthier for your dog to eat two smaller portions, one in the morning and one in the evening.

Your Boxer's feeding should also be scheduled so that you are able to avoid feeding the dog one hour before or after strenuous exercise. Your dog should also have access to fresh, cool water at all times to discourage gulping huge quantities of water immediately before or after eating.

How Much to Feed

Are you feeding your Boxer too much, too little, or just enough? While a puppy is growing and maturing, it is particularly important not to overfeed. Though a roly-poly puppy looks cute, this extra weight could possibly begin the destructive cycle

of hip dysplasia or cause other musculoskeletal problems. Excessively heavy adults and seniors put more strain on their joints as well as their organs. So, be kind; don't overfeed.

It is equally important, especially with puppies, that all of the puppy's nutritional needs are met. If puppies are too thin or are given food that does not provide them with the nutrients they need, the results can be disastrous.

In order to determine if your Boxer is too thin, too fat, or just right, feel the flesh covering your dog's ribs. If you exert slight pressure and can't feel any ribs, your Boxer needs to begin cutting back on his daily intake. (If you're not exercising your Boxer, this can be a factor, too.) If you exert slight pressure and feel the dog's ribs, he is most likely about where he should be on the scale. If you don't even have to push on your dog's sides to feel ribs, you will need to increase your dog's body weight. If a thin dog is eating but not gaining weight, be sure to have your veterinarian rule out that your dog's thinness is not being caused by parasites or disease.

How to Feed

Once you've determined what type of food to feed your dog and when to feed him, you may still have questions as to how to feed him. Some Boxers, if fed dry food, can be allowed to "free feed" without gaining excessive weight. The dog simply takes a nibble here or there from his bowl until by evening the entire helping is finished. Problems that can occur with this feeding method are that if food is left out for long periods of time, it can become stale or infested with bugs; it may attract mice to the dog's dinner bowl; and, of course, there are those Boxers who would eat their entire day's rations in one swift feeding, spending the rest of the day begging for more.

Controlled or rationed feeding is often the better choice for many dogs. In this manner, the dog's total daily allotment of food is divided into two or three servings. The meal is put down only during these scheduled feeding times. To discourage the attraction of insects or other undesirable creatures, many owners pick up whatever food remains after 20 minutes. This is a long enough time to allow your Boxer to leisurely eat his food without making him feel threatened that the bowl is going to be picked up at any time.

Tip: If you have more than one dog, you will need to feed your dogs in their crates. This avoids any unnecessary squabbles between dogs and is one more step required to prevent a grudge from developing between two antagonistic Boxers.

Changing Foods— Gradually

Is your dog not thriving on his current food? If so, make the changeover to a new food, gradually. Sudden changes can cause bouts of diarrhea.

To switch over with a minimal amount of agony, use a 10-day plan: During a period of 10 days, begin substituting larger amounts of the new food in with the dog's old food. For example, the first day, give your Boxer nine parts of "old" food, one part of new food, the second day, eight parts of "old" food, two parts of new food. Continue mixing each day until finally you are feeding all new food.

Chapter Ten
Preventive Care

Your Boxer's good looks alone will not keep him healthy. Regular exercise, fresh water, good-quality food, and frequent brushing all help to cultivate a sleek, muscular Boxer, but scheduled preventive veterinary care will go far in helping your Boxer live well into his senior years.

Veterinary Care

One study found that if an owner has provided his or her dog with little or no veterinary care, it is a sign that an owner is giving up on the dog and he will soon be headed for a shelter because the owner doesn't care what is going to happen to him. Obviously, if you are taking the time to read up on the Boxer and learn about his traits and care requirements, you care. And, you're going to make sure your puppy or adult receives the quality veterinary care he deserves throughout his life.

Regular Care

"My Boxer is healthy. Why do I need to pay a veterinarian to tell me that?" Well, for one thing, peace of mind. As a dog owner, hearing that your new puppy is disease-free is great news. Learning that your adopted adult Boxer has no signs of hip dysplasia and will not suffer from this debilitating disease is great news, too.

But the importance of regular veterinary care goes beyond the value of confirming good or bad health suspicions. It is key in preventing a myriad of diseases that can attack and cripple or kill a healthy Boxer. With the vaccines that are available today, and those that will become available in future years, there is no reason for a Boxer to die of any preventable disease.

For diseases that are not preventable—at least not at this point—regular veterinary care can detect these diseases early and provide either cures or promising treatment. Diseases, however, cannot be detected early if the dog is not seen regularly, at least once a year for adult dogs.

Life with a treasured Boxer is never long enough, so it is crucial that you give your devoted partner the best shot at living a lengthy, healthy, and pain-free life. Make sure you are mentally and financially committed to providing good, regular veterinary care for your Boxer.

Finding the Right Veterinarian

If you have a veterinarian you really like from a previous or current pet, you're lucky. If you recently moved to a new town or this is your first dog and you need to find a veterinarian, there are several ways to go about locating a good one.

• If you live in the same town as your breeder, ask your breeder who he or she uses. If your breeder is from another town, chances are he or she will know someone in your area who can give you some recommendations. If your breeder is inexperienced or you don't value that individual's opinion, you will need to search a bit harder.

• A call to the local humane society or nonprofit shelter may give you some clues as to whom you could use.

• If you have neighbors with healthy dogs, ask them, too.

• If you're really stumped for names, you can call the American Animal Hospital Association (AAHA) at 1-800-252-2242 for the name of a practitioner in your area.

Once you have a few names, you'll probably want to make an appointment with one. If you don't hit it off with this veterinarian, keep looking. It doesn't matter how many advanced degrees and titles trail off after a veterinarian's name, if you're not comfortable talking to him or her about your Boxer, you will never be able to tap into the veterinarian's knowledge and expertise. You should attempt to find a veterinarian you feel you could ask the dumbest dog question in the world and not be embarrassed or uneasy. The truth of the matter is, when it comes to questions regarding your Boxer's health or behavior, there are no dumb questions!

When you find a qualified veterinarian you and your Boxer are comfortable with, congratulations; you've just taken a big step toward keeping your Boxer healthy. Now you need to make sure you keep an appointment each year in order to keep your Boxer current on his vaccinations.

Common Contagious Infections

With the vaccinations that are available today, there is absolutely no reason to expose a puppy or an adult dog to any common killers. There are several viruses that continue to kill puppies and adults in large numbers and it is strongly advised that your Boxer be brought up-to-date on his shots and put on a regular vaccination schedule.

Core vs. Non-core Vaccinations

Vaccinations are divided between those that are recommended for all healthy dogs in all areas of the country (core vaccines) and those that are recommended for dogs with ele-

vated risks of coming in contact with certain diseases (non-core vaccines). Vaccine protocols evolve as diseases become higher and lower risks; what may be listed as a core vaccination today could become a non-core vaccine a decade from now. Additionally, new diseases emerge and may move from the non-core list (as they are initially quite rare) to the core list (as the disease spreads across the country).

The following list is the most current vaccination listing and protocol at press time. It is advisable, however, to stay current with evolving diseases and new vaccines, as well as changing vaccination requirements (i.e., annual booster, a booster every three years, or no boosters needed). Additionally, if the health of your Boxer changes, if he becomes immunocompromised or is ill, it is often considered a greater risk to the dog's health to vaccinate for any disease while he is in a weakened state. Your veterinarian will be able to counsel you on the risks of vaccination at this time.

Core Vaccines

Currently, vaccinations generally recommended for all Boxer puppies include: canine parvovirus, canine distemper, canine adenovirus-2, and rabies. Parvovirus and distemper are both highly contagious and can spread rapidly among unvaccinated puppies.

Parvo attacks the pup's gastrointestinal tract, causing fever, vomiting, diarrhea, and often death within

Allergic Reactions

Boxers have been known to suffer allergic reactions to vaccinations. With the advances in vaccines, less allergic reactions are seen today than in years past. The two vaccines most likely to produce an adverse reaction are the rabies vaccine and a non-core vaccine for leptospirosis.

Regardless of what vaccines your Boxer is receiving, it is advisable to be aware of the symptoms of an allergic reaction and know what to do while traveling back to your veterinarian. Note that a mild reaction may progress rapidly to a serious, life-threatening condition within a matter of minutes. At the first sign of a reaction, call your veterinarian.

Mild reaction: slight fever; tiredness that generally resolves itself.

Moderate reaction: itchiness; *slight* swelling around eyes and mouth.

Serious reaction: anaphylaxis—throat swells shut; seizures, cardiac arrest, rapid drop in blood pressure; death.

What to do: treatment of an adverse reaction involves the administration of an antihistamine. Your veterinarian can advise you of the exact dosage of Benedryl that should be given to your Boxer. Pills can be difficult to administer if a dog is uncomfortable or is swelling quickly; keep a packet of quick-dissolving Benadryl strips handy for use. These strips work simply by placing them on your dog's tongue; no swallowing is needed.

Future vaccinations: If your Boxer has experienced an allergic reaction, your veterinarian will either eliminate the vaccine from your dog's protocol (if it's a non-core vaccine) or make sure the dog has had enough antihistamine before receiving the vaccination that he won't experience a severe reaction. The Boxer will be required to stay in the clinic for a set amount of time to ensure that no adverse reaction is taking place whenever he is vaccinated in the future, too.

48 to 72 hours following the onset of symptoms. (The onset of any of these symptoms in a puppy—even one who is receiving vaccinations—requires an immediate trip to the veterinarian.) The parvovirus is exceptionally virulent—living for long periods of time on virtually any surface—and is resistant to cold, heat, humidity, and aridity. To become infected, the puppy doesn't have to come in direct contact with a sick dog; rather, a family member can step on an area that has the virus and bring it into the home on the bottom of his or her shoe.

Canine distemper attacks the respiratory, gastrointestinal, and

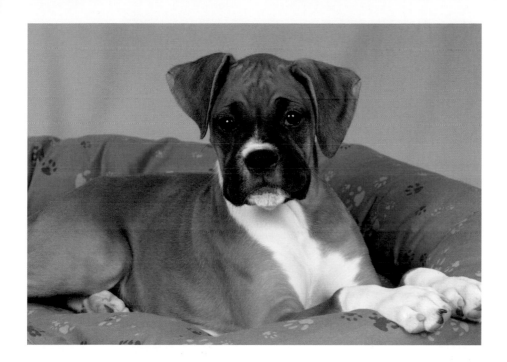

nervous systems of puppies, with early symptoms including: fever, nasal and eye discharge, coughing, vomiting, diarrhea, and possibly seizures and paralysis. Symptoms are so varied and the disease is so deadly, that if a puppy shows any signs of illness, he should be taken to the veterinarian *immediately.* Exposure is usually airborne, and pups can get this disease from infected puppies and dogs, as well as wild canids (fox, wolves, coyotes), raccoons, skunks, and ferrets.

Canine adenovirus has two forms that can affect puppies. The adenovirus-1 causes canine hepatitis, a virus that invades the pup's liver, causing cell damage, hemorrhaging, and often death. The ade-

novirus-2 is a major cause of infectious tracheobronchitis, or kennel cough. The vaccine for canine adenovirus-2 provides the puppy protection from the adenovirus-2 virus, as well as providing cross-protection against adenovirus-1.

Rabies is a deadly virus that attacks the nervous system and can be transmitted to both animals and humans. The virus is secreted in the saliva of a rabid animal and the most common mode of transmission is through a bite. A less common but entirely possible mode of transmission of the disease can occur if the rabid animal's saliva comes in contact with the person or animal's eyes, nose, or mouth, or an open cut on the skin. Once the virus is in an unvaccinated animal's or human's system, the disease is fatal. The most common exposure by a dog to rabies is through exposure to rabid skunks, raccoons, coyotes, bats, or foxes. Domestic cats have been increasingly reported with rabies as many owners do not vaccinate their pets and yet allow the felines outdoors where they come in contact with rabid wildlife. The rabies vaccine is required for all dogs by state, local, or provincial law.

Core Vaccine Protocol

A minimum of three doses of the parvovirus, distemper, and aden-ovirus-2 vaccines are given three to four weeks apart, beginning at the age of six to eight weeks. One year after the series is completed, the puppy receives a booster vaccination. Following that vaccination, the Boxer only needs revaccination every three years or longer, depending on the advice of your veterinarian.

The initial rabies vaccine is administered as early as three months, and then is followed up with a second vaccination one year after the initial vaccine. Additional vaccination for rabies is given according to local, state, or provincial law, and may be either annually or every three years. Your veterinarian will be aware of local laws and will advise you.

Non-core Vaccines

Canine Infectious Respiratory Disease Complex (CIRDC) causes sneezing, nasal and eye discharge, and possibly lower respiratory disease. It is called a "complex" because generally there are several diseases at work at one time, including both viral and bacterial diseases. CIRDC is commonly referred to as "kennel cough," as areas in which many dogs are kept in close contact are where this complex of diseases is most easily spread. The **Bordetella vaccine** is recommended for puppies and dogs who will be exposed to many other dogs, and the vaccine is required by most boarding facilities. The vaccine is given initially in two doses, four weeks apart, with a booster annually. Duration of immunity (the amount of time the Boxer is protected) is from nine to 12 months; however, dogs in high-risk environments may be revaccinated every six months.

Canine influenza virus is a form of canine flu that was first seen in Greyhounds in 2004–2005. In 2008, the disease, which causes coughing, fever, and nasal discharge, had been confirmed in 28 states. The vaccination for the canine influenza virus, which was released in May 2009, is currently recommended only for dogs at highest risk of coming in contact with the virus: dogs who participate in activities with many other dogs present (e.g., dog shows, obedience trials, training classes, or traveling with their owners), or dogs who are boarded on occasion. This recommendation may change, however. Depending on how common the virus becomes, the vaccine may move from the non-core or optional vaccination list to the core or recommended vaccination list. **Note:** Many boarding facilities require this vaccination along with the *Bordetella* vaccine for all boarders.

Leptospirosis is a disease caused by several forms of the *Leptospira* bacterium, which is shed in the urine of infected animals. Symptoms of Leptospirosis include fever, weakness, vomiting, abdominal pain, and kidney or liver failure. This vaccine carries a high risk of acute anaphylaxis in puppies under the age of 12 weeks and toy breeds; however, severe allergic reactions are possible in larger adult dogs, too. This vaccine should only be given if your veterinarian determines your Boxer's exposure risk is high for this disease, and annual vaccination should be discontinued as soon as the risk for exposure has been reduced.

Lyme disease is caused by the bite of an infected tick carrying the bacteria *Borrelia burgdorferi*. Early disease symptoms usually don't show up until two to six months after exposure to the bacteria and can include fever, lethargy, and appetite loss, along with lameness. Antibiotics are very adept at treating Lyme disease, and the preferred mode of prevention continues to be topical tick repellent products. The vaccine for Lyme disease is recommended only for dogs who are in an area of known high risk or those who will be traveling to an area where the disease is endemic. The vaccine is given initially in two doses two to four weeks apart, and then an annual revaccination just prior to the start of tick season.

Periodontal disease vaccine is a relatively new vaccine that was developed to prevent and control periodontal disease in dogs. The vaccine includes inactivated bacterin: *P. denticanis, P. gulae,* and *P. salivosa*, which are thought to play a role in periodontitis in the dog. The inactivated bacterin are thought to enhance the dog's immune response to these naturally occurring bacteria and lessen the advancement of periodontal disease. The vaccine is initially given in two doses three weeks apart, followed by subsequent doses in six- or 12-month intervals. The efficacy of this product had not been determined as of 2010. Boxer owners should watch for updates on this vaccine—if it *is* effective, it could be helpful in dealing with the Boxer's somewhat difficult dental health, particularly as the Boxer ages.

Internal Parasites

Boxers of all ages can become infected with one or more types of worms and/or protozoa. The most common intestinal worms include: hookworms, roundworms, tapeworms, and whipworms. The most common form of protozoa that affects dogs is *Giardia*; however, there are other less common types that can also cause serious illness. And, of course, Boxers in all areas of North America are susceptible to the deadly heartworm.

Intestinal Worms

Virtually every Boxer will eventually suffer an infection from one type or another of intestinal worms. Your veterinarian will require annual fecal exams to search for an infestation of worms; however, if you notice a change in appetite, weight loss, coughing, diarrhea, a rough or dry coat, or if you think something just isn't right with your Boxer, have him examined by your veterinarian. Worms are relatively easy to treat and usually require a few days of medication followed by a re-exam of the dog's stools. It is essential during treatment to clean up after your dog immediately upon defecation and to keep your yard immaculate to prevent re-infection.

Tip: Most oral heartworm preventives provide a preventive for several types of intestinal worms.

Protozoa

The two most commonly seen intestinal protozoa are *Coccidia* and *Giardia*. These parasites both tend to damage the intestinal lining, causing rather explosive, watery stools often mixed with blood. The most immediate danger from protozoa is that the dog loses more fluids through his stools than he can replace by drinking, becoming seriously dehydrated. Treatment for *Coccidia* stops the parasite from multiplying and gives the infected dog's immune system time to kill the remaining parasites. Medications for *Giardia* eliminate the protozoa from the dog's system. Both protozoa are highly contagious, so multiple pet families need to sanitize all surfaces, as well as practice good hygiene themselves, since the protozoa can infect people, too.

Heartworm

With as much publicity as this parasite has received, and with the advent of such simple means to prevent infestations, it is still somewhat amazing that so many puppies and dogs have serious, life-threatening cases of heartworm. In the past, heartworm was only prevalent in some areas of the country, and only a concern in the warmest months when mosquitoes—the insect that transmits this awful condition—are at their peak. This is no longer the case, as heartworm infections are now seen throughout North America and in most areas can be contracted year-round.

Heartworms are transmitted to dogs when a mosquito carrying infective heartworm larvae injects the larvae into a dog's bloodstream while taking its blood meal. During the first 90 days in the dog's body, the larvae work their way into the blood vessels of the lungs. Here, the growing worm matures over a period of three months, reaching lengths of up to 14 inches. Mature worms damage the blood vessels, which in turn reduces the heart's ability to function. Severe heart and lung disease ensue.

To add insult to injury, adult worms mate and produce new microfilariae, which can cause a severe immune reaction within the dog, damaging internal organs. If a mosquito bites a dog with microfilariae, the microfilariae develop into infective larvae within the mosquito within ten to 14 days. If the mosquito bites another dog, this dog is now infected, and the cycle continues.

Treatment involves a substantial risk for the infected dog. Secondary problems that can occur from the dying of worms in the lungs include an inflammatory reaction that may also need to be treated. Surgical removal of heartworms is extremely high-risk, but in some cases necessary.

Prevention is simplest and most effective. Heartworm preventives can be given as an oral pill or tablet, a topical liquid that is squeezed from a tube onto the dog's skin (on the back), or as an injection (your veterinarian will need to give your dog this injection). Some heartworm preventives are broad-spectrum in that they also contain ingredients that kill fleas, ticks, and/or intestinal parasites.

Before your veterinarian prescribes a heartworm preventive, he or she will give your dog a blood test to check for the presence of adult heartworms. This test is given annually.

External Parasites

In addition to internal parasites, your Boxer can have external parasites as well. These pests usually are most prevalent in the summer months, but in warm areas of the country, they can be a problem year-round.

Fleas

It's no wonder that these blood-sucking parasites have been around relatively unchanged since prehistoric times. Fleas have survived through the ages because they are resilient, adaptable, and difficult to eradicate. They have been the scourge of mankind and dog- and catdom and have been the carriers of diseases and the cause of many deaths. Besides hurting when they bite, fleas transmit a host of infectious diseases (remember the Black Plague of medieval times?), pass tapeworm infections, and can cause serious allergic reactions. Heavy infestations of fleas can literally drain a small puppy of a substantial quantity of blood.

In addition to causing problems with your dog, fleas can also quickly take over a home. If the fleas have a steady source of food (your Boxer), they will rapidly mature and begin reproducing—laying eggs on your

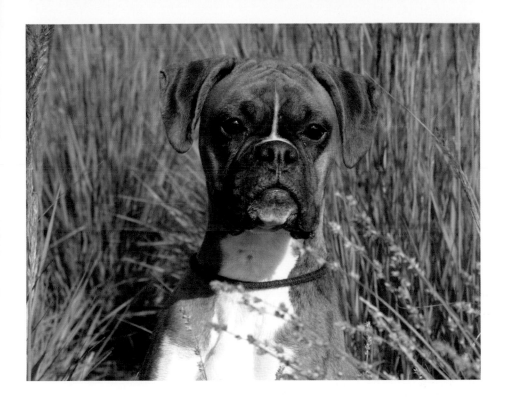

dog, in your rugs, carpets, couches, chairs, and beds. In a short time, a small flea problem can multiply rapidly.

Prevention: Flea prevention is the best solution. There are several products on the market already, with more on the way, that kill adult fleas before they are able to reproduce.

At least one product on the market prevents flea eggs and larvae from developing and is used in conjunction with an "adulticide" that kills adult fleas.

Flea preventives include both topical applications (a small tube of preventive is applied to the skin between the dog's shoulders), oral medications (monthly chewable pills), and flea collars. Many flea preventives also include preventives for ticks; however, some products are strictly for keeping a dog flea-free. Some heartworm preventives also include protection against fleas. Flea preventives are sold both over-the-counter and by your veterinarian in prescriptions.

Note: Adverse reactions to flea and tick topical applications that were reported in 2009 prompted a collaborative technical evaluation and review of all topical flea products by the Environmental Protection Agency (EPA) and Health Canada. A report was anticipated to be released by EPA in early 2010 with possible regulatory action. For the safety of your Boxer, stay abreast of issues such as this with your veterinarian.

If your dog is already infested with fleas and you fear the worst—that fleas are in your home—most veterinarians recommend a three-pronged approach to ridding your home and dog of the fleas. The key is that the dog and his environment (inside and outside) need to be treated at the same time. If you only rid your dog of its fleas, when the eggs in the carpet hatch the following week, they'll be back. So, treat your house, the dog's bed, carpeted areas, and anywhere else your dog frequents at the same time you treat your dog. If your yard is infested with fleas, you will need to consider ways to approach this problem as well. Make sure you consult your veterinarian before using any pesticides, however, because these chemicals can be more toxic to your dog than to the fleas you're trying to kill.

You will need to treat your home and dog more than once, too. There is no one product that is capable of wiping out all life stages of the flea at the same time. Therefore, as the eggs hatch, you will need to re-treat your house and dog. Follow your veterinarian's advice carefully and your flea problems should be squashed. Once the fleas are gone, maintain a flea preventive to keep fleas off your Boxer at all times.

Ticks

As discussed earlier in this chapter, ticks can be the carriers of deadly organisms that can affect not only dogs but humans as well. Ticks are hosts to Lyme disease, Rocky Mountain spotted fever, babesiosis, and ehrlichiosis. They can also cause a severe reaction in dogs who are sensitive to the tick's saliva, from swelling to paralysis. Tick bites can also be deep and develop into a secondary bacterial infection.

Fortunately, ticks are easy to spot on the Boxer's smooth coat. If you find a tick, remove it immediately with tweezers, grasping the tick as close to the head as possible, and pulling straight out without twisting. Leaving the head in can cause an infection. Destroy the tick by crushing it or dropping it into a cup filled with alcohol, gasoline, or turpentine. If you suspect the tick might be a carrier of a disease—if you're in an area where Lyme disease is prevalent—save the tick's body in a reclosable plastic bag and take it to your veterinarian for testing.

Meanwhile, wash your dog's bite area with soap and water and apply an antiseptic. If your dog has never been bitten by a tick before, watch for an allergic reaction. If the dog reacts with hives or begins to swell around the throat area, rush him to the veterinarian; this type of allergic reaction may cut off the dog's breathing.

Prevention: A vaccination for one tick-borne disease, Lyme disease, is available for disease prevention (see page 145); however, it is not 100 percent effective, nor does it protect against other tickborne diseases. The vaccination also does not prevent adult ticks from taking blood meals on your dog. The best way to avoid a tick infestation is to apply a topical or oral medication specifically for ticks. Some heartworm medications also include a tick preventive. Talk to your veterinarian about the possibility of using one of these products during tick season.

Mites

Of the various types of mites—there are several—demodex mites tend to cause the greatest problems among Boxers. The mites live in the dog's hair follicles and sebaceous glands. Demodectic or red mange causes a red, hairless condition. Sometimes Boxer puppies will develop small spots of demodectic mange during teething, possibly linked to the stress of this stage. If the mange cannot be controlled with medications, an improved diet, and perhaps the reduction of the dog's stress, some breeders feel this may be a sign of a more compromised immune system. Mange is not something that you want to see progress if you can avoid it. Work with your veterinarian to help rectify the situation.

Chapter Eleven

Common Diseases of the Boxer

Every breed has particular health problems that seem to crop up more frequently than in other breeds. The Boxer is no different. Though robust in build and strong in mind, the Boxer's health can be crippled by a variety of diseases. Depending on the source, the Boxer has been identified as being at a higher risk as a breed for 26 to 50 different diseases, depending on the source. Some of these diseases are fatal; others are debilitating but not life-threatening, and still others are chronic conditions, some of which can be treated (but not cured), and others that have no known treatment. Though this sounds like a daunting list of possible health problems (virtually all of which are costly to diagnose and treat), the good news is that with the well-bred Boxer, *most* of these diseases and conditions are relatively rare. With careful breeding, health screenings and tests, and accurate record keeping, it is the continued goal of conscientious breeders that the occurrence of most of the Boxer's hereditary diseases are low.

Unfortunately, as the Boxer maintains its position as one of the most popular breeds in North America, the rate of these inherited diseases is expected to climb among those breeders who simply don't care or are unaware of the health of the Boxers they are producing. For this reason, it behooves the future puppy owner to research the breed's common health problems and understand how to test for certain diseases and record the results on a puppy's pedigree. For the owner of an adult Boxer, it is also invaluable to know what types of problems could occur and what kinds of actions can be taken.

Life-threatening Diseases

The most common diseases and conditions that can prove deadly to the Boxer include: bloat, several forms of cancer, degenerative myelopathy, heat stroke, heart disease, and histiocytic ulcerative colitis.

With these diseases and conditions, it is important to recognize early warning signs in order to give your Boxer the highest chance of survival, or at a minimum, the greatest amount of comfort and pain control.

Bloat

Bloat is the common name for Gastric Dilation-Volvulus (GDV), in which the dog's stomach becomes distended with gas and begins to twist. As the stomach twists, the flow of gas, fluids, and food from the stomach to the intestines is blocked. The blood supply to the stomach is also cut off. If a dog can be seen by a veterinarian immediately at the onset of this syndrome, he may have a chance for survival. However, if the twisting and strangling of the stomach and intestines are not halted immediately, the Boxer will die in a few hours.

Symptoms of bloat: If your Boxer bloats, you have virtually minutes to get help. Knowing what the symptoms of the syndrome are may mean the difference between saving your Boxer or not.

• Uneasiness, restlessness, inability to lie down comfortably
• Repeated nonproductive attempts to vomit
• Drooling
• Breathing rapidly but not deeply
• Gums that are either very pale, very red, or blue
• A bloated or distended appearance to the stomach area

Prevention: The possible causes of GDV have been studied for more than a decade, but little conclusive evidence is available. There are no clear-cut indications of which Boxers may be more susceptible to bloat than others, making the onset of GDV something that cannot be predicted with any accuracy. Within the past decade, however, several key studies *do* give some ideas as to why some Boxers may suffer from bloat. These indicators include:

• Dogs who are fed one large, single meal a day
• Dogs who eat their meals rapidly
• Dogs who are fearful or stressed
• Male dogs may be at higher risk
• Dry foods containing an oil or fat (e.g., sunflower oil, animal fat) listed as one of the first four ingredients

Based on the current information on GDV, here are suggestions to help prevent your Boxer from suffering from bloat:

• Feed two or more small meals a day rather than one huge meal.
• Place rubber chew toys in the dog's food to keep him from gulping his meal too fast.
• Allow constant access to cool, fresh water to avoid gulping large quantities.
• Do not feed a Boxer who has recently exercised or is going to exercise. Allow one hour for the dog to cool down after exercising before feeding. If the dog is going to exercise after eating, feed only a small portion of the meal at least one hour before the exercise. The balance of the meal can be fed an hour after the exercise is completed.

• Keep abreast of the latest developments in prevention and treatment of this disease. As research is completed, the techniques recommended to avoid bloat may change. Your veterinarian will be a good source for this information.

Cancer

Boxers continue to suffer from a greater rate of cancer than virtually any other breed of dog. As a breed, Boxers have exhibited a predisposition to brain tumors, hemangiosarcomas, lymphomas, mast cell tumors, and osteosarcomas. Research is underway for several types of cancer in an effort to determine genetic links; however, testing that would enable breeders to determine which Boxers *had* the disease, which dogs were carriers of the disease, and which Boxers were genetically free of disease is still in the future. In the meantime, it is critical that breeders track the occurrences of cancer in their lines, not only with the dogs they own and breed, but also their dogs' offspring.

Tip: A quality breeder will openly share his or her cancer-tracking efforts with you, as well as any information on Boxer-specific research being performed on these types of cancers. Most breeders experiencing cancer in their lines will participate in the genetic research by sending tumor and blood samples of affected dogs, and blood samples of healthy Boxers that are free of disease and older than eight years old.

Brain tumors: As a brachycephalic (short-nosed) breed, the Boxer is at a higher risk of a glioma, or brain tumor, than other longer-nosed breeds. The tumors range from slow-growth benign tumors to high-grade, aggressive tumors. A research team at North Carolina State University is studying what causes the tumors to grow in the hopes that they can target the growth factors associated with the tumors and develop effective treatment options.

In Boxers, gliomas are most often seen in older dogs. Symptoms vary depending on where the tumor is located, but can include seizures, changes in behavior, head tilting, rapid flicking of the eyes, unsteadiness or clumsiness, circling, and difficulty swallowing.

Diagnosis is costly and includes a CT scan, and either a CT-biopsy or a surgical biopsy (sample of the mass) to determine what type of treatment may be effective. Current treatment options include prednisone (to reduce fluid around the tumor and reduce symptoms *temporarily*) and radiation (to slow the growth of the tumor and extend the dog's life). Chemotherapy has not proven very effective; however, different chemicals are being studied.

Surgery is also difficult because in order to remove the tumor, healthy brain matter must also be removed.

Hemangiosarcomas: This type of cancer affects the cells lining the dog's blood vessels, usually in the bladder, bone, brain, kidneys, muscles, oral cavity, spleen, and the lining of the abdominal cavity (peritoneum). Hemangiosarcoma is a very aggressive cancer. If discovered early, surgery and chemotherapy may extend a Boxer's life by seven to eight months. Usually, this form of cancer has few symptoms in the early stages and isn't discovered until it has metastasized and is in its advanced stages. At this point, the tumor is resistant to most available treatments.

Symptoms can vary depending on where the tumor is located and where the cancer spreads, but the first signs that Boxer owners typically cite are lethargy and a general malaise.

Research is currently focused on the development of an early detection test for this type of cancer and a therapeutic cancer vaccine.

Lymphosarcoma: This is a very common cancer in dogs and an even more common cancer in Boxers. Lymphosarcoma (or lymphoma) affects the lymphocytes (a type of white blood cell) and the lymphoid tissues (found in lymph nodes, bone marrow, gastrointestinal tract, liver, and spleen). Where the disease begins determines the type of lymphoma and the earliest symptoms of this disease. The most common form affects the lymph nodes, causing the dog to initially appear tired or suffer a loss of appetite. More advanced signs may include breathing difficulties, diarrhea, excessive thirst and urination, vomiting, and weakness.

Chemotherapy continues to be the mode of treatment for lymphoma, and is reported to have up to 80 percent success in enabling dogs to go into remission (the disappearance of *detectable* cancer). The average remission time is from eight to 10 months, giving the dog roughly a year extension of a good, quality life.

Mast cell tumors: This type of tumor can arise anywhere in the body where mast cells are found, but most frequently occur in the Boxer in the skin. Boxers are considered to be at an exceptionally high risk for this form of cancer. Unfortunately, in addition to being disfiguring and painful, mast cell tumors are also invasive and difficult to treat. Typically, a Boxer owner will notice a lump in the dog's skin. A good approach is to have the lump immediately aspirated (a small sample removed with a needle) to determine if it is perhaps a benign fatty tumor or lipoma that is also commonly found in Boxers.

If the tumor is determined to be a mast cell tumor, its stage and location largely determine how successful treatments can be. Also, some tumors seem to be very slow-growing, whereas others spread rapidly.

When a Boxer owner discovers a lump, the greatest chance for success is to receive early diagnosis and treatment. This is not a tumor you would want to "wait and see" what it does. Treatments include surgery and chemotherapy.

Osteosarcomas: This cancer typically strikes breeds that weigh more than 88 pounds; however, the Boxer is unfortunate in that it has a higher risk of developing the disease than most other breeds its size. Osteosarcoma most frequently affects the long bones of the legs, with common sites of disease starting in the stifle (rear leg knee), the hock, the shoulder, and the distal radius (similar to the wrist in humans). Though these are the most common sites, osteosarcoma *can* affect other bones.

Symptoms usually appear as a swelling and an area that is tender or painful to the touch for the dog. An owner may also feel heat emanating from the swollen area. Diagnosis is made through X-rays of the bones, as well as the dog's lungs, where the cancer may spread in more advanced stages.

The goal of treatment for this aggressive cancer is "palliative" or to provide comfort (pain relief) and to slow the spread of the cancer. Treatments include amputation, chemotherapy, and radiation.

Degenerative Myelopathy

Degenerative Myelopathy (DM) was first discovered in the early 1970s. At that time it was considered to be a degenerative, immune-related neurological disease limited to German Shepherd dogs. Unfortunately, in the past decade, it has become obvious that they were not the only breed that suffers from this debilitating disease, and that on that short list of dog breeds is the Boxer.

DM is similar to multiple sclerosis in humans. Basically, the Boxer's own immune system attacks his nervous system, damaging neural tissue—beginning in the chest region of the spinal cord. When this tissue is damaged, the brain can no longer communicate movement commands or receive sensory information from the rear limbs of the dog. DM usually occurs in older Boxers around the age of seven or eight; however, symptoms can occur earlier or later.

Researchers at the University of Missouri-Columbia College of Veterinary Medicine discovered a genetic mutation that causes dogs to be at risk for developing DM. In 2008, a test was developed that clearly identifies dogs who are *clear* of the mutated gene (have two normal copies of the gene), those who are carriers (one normal, one mutated copy), and those dogs who are at highest risk of developing DM (both genes are mutated). With this genetic test, it is now possible to eradicate this disease from the Boxer breed—if breeders test their dogs for the mutated genes.

Early symptoms of DM include an apparent weakness in the rear end, knuckling over (dragging of knuckles on floor), and loss of sensation in the dog's rear toes and feet.

Unfortunately, there is no known cure for DM. Exercise, such as walking and swimming, may help to maintain muscles and circulation. Other measures include physical rehabilitation, pressure sore prevention, keeping an eye out for urinary infections, and improving the Boxer's mobility through the use of walking aids, such as dog carts, slings, and special harnesses.

Heart Diseases

There are two forms of heart disease that plague the Boxer: ARVC and subvalvular aortic stenosis. Both are hereditary diseases that, with testing, careful recordkeeping, and wise breeding practices could be lessened substantially in frequency.

ARVC: Formerly known as "Boxer cardiomyopathy," arrhythmogenic right ventricular cardiomyopathy (ARVC) is a heart disease that is frequently fatal and generally strikes without warning when the Boxer is exercising or is excited. It can also occur when the Boxer is completely at rest. Boxers have the highest incidence of this form of heart disease. It is not a disease of the old; ARVC is frequently seen in Boxers less than one year of age.

Many dogs do not show any signs of the disease until they die suddenly and unexpectedly. Other dogs may show symptoms such as fainting or weakness after exercise. In some cases, the dog's heart may become enlarged.

Over time, the heart of a Boxer suffering from ARVC experiences structural changes. The heart can become solid and dense, with fibrous fatty tissues infiltrating the heart muscles, causing them in turn to stretch and become filled with holes. Diagnosis is through a combination of veterinary diagnostic tools. Previously, the only way to determine if a Boxer had ARVC was through an electrocardiogram (ECG) using a Holter Monitor, which records the ECG for a 24-hour period.

A second way to determine if an asymptomatic Boxer has the disease—or possesses the genes to develop the disease—is through a genetic test developed in 2009 by researcher Kathryn Meurs, DVM, of Washington State University College of Veterinary Medicine. With a swab of the Boxer's cheek or a blood sample, it can be determined if the dog possesses two mutated genes (has the highest risk for ARVC), one mutated and one normal gene (a carrier of ARVC), or has two normal genes (free of disease). If a Boxer carries the causative mutation, further testing with the Holter Monitor would be in line.

Tip: Not all dogs with a set of mutated genes may develop ARVC. There is extreme variation in the disease, and some dogs who have the mutated genes will never show signs of ARVC, whereas others with the causative mutation will be very affected by ARVC. This means that there are other genes that impact how severely a dog will or won't demonstrate the disease.

If ARVC is diagnosed early, it often can be managed with medications, allowing the Boxer to live a full life. Medications currently cost less than $100/month.

Subaortic stenosis: Subaortic stenosis (SAS) is an often fatal heart disease that, unfortunately, is seen in significant numbers in a handful of breeds, including the Boxer. SAS is believed to have a genetic basis, and studies are underway to locate the gene pair responsible for this devastating disease.

So what exactly is SAS? This heart disease involves a blockage at or below the aortic valve. If the narrowing of the aorta is severe enough, the blood flow from the heart is restricted. To compensate, the heart's left side works harder to push the blood through the narrow vessel. This increased work makes the laboring side of the heart become overworked and enlarged.

Often the first sign of SAS is a slight murmur in a puppy's heart. The effects of an aortic obstruction can be noticeable when the affected Boxer is quite young. Weakness and fainting are symptoms of the disease, but puppies have been known to literally "drop dead." Detection of the

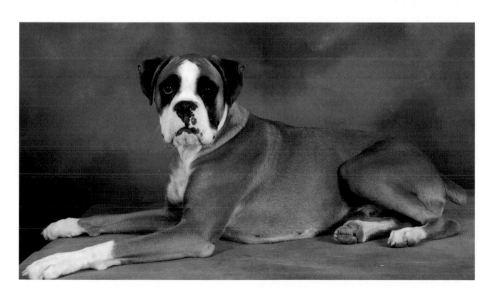

disease can be made with a thorough veterinary exam, including radiographs of the heart, and a diagnosis confirmed through the use of an ultrasound.

Current treatment methods typically strive to allow the Boxer with SAS to have a more normal exercise tolerance and life span. Beta blockers are used to keep the heart from racing and have been shown to improve the survival rate by three years over dogs receiving no treatment.

Heatstroke: Brachycephalic or short-nosed breeds may be able to breathe better than a long-nosed dog when holding an attacker's arm; however, the selective breeding that produced this bite and short muzzle also produced a breed that does not tolerate heat well at all. Dogs cool themselves by panting. Longer-nosed dogs are able to cool themselves much more efficiently than short-nosed breeds.

Signs of heatstroke include rapid panting, weakness, tiredness, an elevated temperature (above 105°F [40.6°C]), dark red to purple gums and tongue, and even disorientation. The dog may also be dehydrated, which can be determined by pinching his skin above his shoulders and observing how quickly it returns to its normal shape. Have your veterinarian show you in advance what "healthy" skin looks like and practice the pinch.

If the Boxer has become overheated, move him quickly to a shady spot and soak with cool, not cold, water. Transport the dog to the vet-erinarian as quickly as possible. Heatstroke can be prevented by minimizing your Boxer's activities in high temperatures and keeping a close eye on him in warmer weather. A Boxer should never be left outdoors for any period of time, especially during the summer. Cool, fresh water should be available at all times, as well as a shady, comfortable spot.

Histiocytic ulcerative colitis: Boxers are susceptible to this disease with such frequency that some experts refer to it as "Boxer ulcerative colitis." The disease is believed to be genetic and is best avoided by studying breed lines that have tracked the disease's occurrence.

In general, colitis is an inflammation of the colon. With Boxers, there is a tendency to develop deep ulcers in the colon wall, making the disease particularly painful. Defecation is abnormal with this disease, often diarrhetic. The stools may contain mucus and some blood.

Because the Boxer tends to develop deep ulcerations, the colitis becomes more than an inconvenient irritation. Treatments to help control the disease and offer some comfort to the dog include strict diets of bland foods, sulfa-containing drugs such as sulfasalazine (commonly used in humans with ulcerative colitis) to help control the symptoms of chronic colitis, and steroids, such as prednisone, to help calm serious inflammation. There is no known cure for the disease, which can progress until it reaches the point of becoming painfully relentless.

Diagnosis is made from intestinal biopsies.

Non-life-threatening Diseases

The following diseases are not life-threatening to the Boxer, but they do appear in Boxers with some regularity. For this reason, Boxer owners should be aware of them and be knowledgeable of the symptoms of the diseases so that prompt, expert veterinary treatment can be provided.

Acne

In many breeds of dogs, acne is a puppy problem. With Boxers, this unsightly problem can extend into adulthood. As with humans, acne in Boxers is caused by clogging in the dog's hair follicles or pores. The acne appears on the dog's chin, often around the time the puppy begins to develop hormonally or during his teen months (eight to 18 months). Treatment for dog acne is much the same as with humans. Acne-cleansing pads are sometimes prescribed to clear the dog's pores. Warm soaks can help to pull the infection from the pores. In more severe cases, a veterinarian may prescribe topical scrubs, gels, or creams.

Allergies

The Boxer is a breed that is thought to have a genetic susceptibility to allergies. Common environmental causes for allergies include many of the same things that give

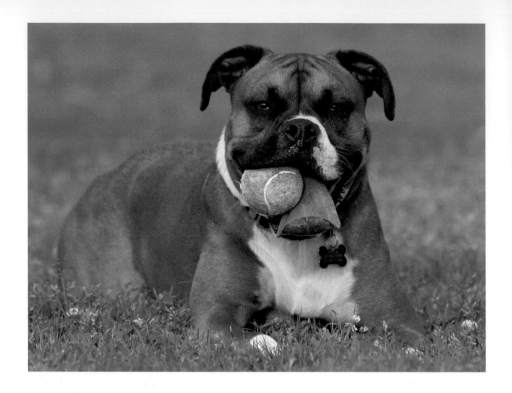

humans fits: pollen, dust mites, various grasses, leaf mold, etc. Additionally, some Boxers are highly allergic to fleas; a single bite can produce an itching, scratching, uncomfortable dog. Food allergies are seen in some Boxers; however, this form of allergy is not as common.

Dogs usually do not react in the same way to allergens as humans; they rarely suffer from runny noses, sneezing, and scratchy eyes. Usually, a dog suffering from allergies will lick the pads of his feet, chew on his knuckles, rub his face, and/or scratch his belly or under his front legs. Severe allergic reactions can trigger ear infections in one or both

ears that require immediate veterinary attention. Chronic allergies can cause skin infections, too.

The Boxer typically responds to allergens—whether fleas, airborne or food borne—with itchy, scaly skin, and/or ear infections. Usually a veterinarian will prescribe something to immediately aid in lessening your Boxer's discomfort—antihistamines, steroids, cyclosporine, or topical medications may be prescribed, as well as medicated shampoos.

If the Boxer doesn't improve (and flea allergies have been ruled out), your veterinarian will want to eliminate the possibility that your Boxer's discomfort stems from food allergies. To clear the most common food ingredients that cause allergic reactions, your veterinarian will have you feed your Boxer a hypoallergenic food for six weeks and then gradually introduce individual proteins and grains.

If food allergies are ruled out and the problem recurs, allergy testing by a specialist is probably in order. If the allergen (or allergens) can be determined, but the source of the allergens cannot be eliminated from the Boxer's environment, then the dog may be a good candidate for immunotherapy.

Corneal Ulcers

The cornea is a very thin covering over the pupil and iris of the eye. It is less than 1 mm thick and is made up of many even thinner layers. With corneal ulcers, one or more layers of the cornea deteriorate, potentially causing severe infection and great pain. With Boxers it gets even worse: the corneal ulcer either heals poorly or doesn't heal at all because of an abnormality seen in the Boxer's cornea, potentially causing a shallow ulcer to become a deep ulcer that can cause the eye to rupture. Since this condition was first seen in the Boxer, it is frequently referred to as "Boxer ulcers."

Symptoms of a corneal ulcer include excessive watering in the eye, blinking, eye discharge, reddening of the whites of the eye (scleritis), inflammation of the pink tissues (conjunctivitis), and sensitivity to bright light. Treatment ranges from topical antibiotics (if the ulcer is caught in the early stages), to one of several types of surgery (e.g., periodic epithelial debridement, anterior stromal puncture, grid keratotomy, and superficial keratectomy).

Cushing's Syndrome

Also referred to as hyperadrenocorticism, Cushing's syndrome is a disease in which the pituitary gland causes an excess of cortisol to be produced in the body. In some cases, a malfunction of the adrenal glands may also cause the rise in cortisol. Tumors on either gland are often the culprit.

Symptoms of the disease vary but often include symptoms similar to diabetes: excessive thirst, appetite, and increased urination. Boxers suffering from the disease may also appear lethargic or suffer hair loss. Diagnosis for the disease can be made through a variety of available screening tests.

Treatment for Cushing's syndrome depends on the source of the disease. Pituitary disease is often treated with medications; adrenal disease may require surgery.

Demodectic Mange

Demodectic mange is caused by an infestation of demodex mites. Though this doesn't sound as if it is a "disease" but rather a pest problem, the cause of "red mange" is believed to be linked with immune-related disease. Demodex mites are normally found in small numbers inhabiting a healthy dog's hair follicles and oil glands. When the Boxer's immune system is compromised, the number of mites takes off, creating an infestation.

The Boxer reacts to the enormous number of mites with hair loss and reddening of the skin. The condition is very uncomfortable, and if left untreated, the Boxer's relentless scratching can cause serious and sometimes fatal bacterial infections. Symptoms can be treated with a variety of methods, including antibiotics, prescription shampoos, dips, an injectable wormer, and other medications. Until the Boxer's immune system is healthy again, the

mites can continue to be a chronic problem.

Ear Infections

Whether your Boxer's ears are cropped or natural, chances are he may suffer an ear infection sometime in his life. Ear infections are most commonly caused by allergies, followed by foreign bodies in the ear. Both conditions can cause an imbalance in the bacteria and yeast naturally found in the dog's ear. Cropped ears do not provide a hedge against getting an infection; in fact, the upright ears may enable foreign bodies such as burrs and other vegetation to lodge themselves deeply in the ear. Pendulous "natural" ears *do not* cause infections; however, the warmer, moister environment of the natural ear may increase the rate that the infection, which started for *other* reasons, grows.

Ear infections generally can be detected early by regularly smelling the dog's ears. An infection will be foul smelling and strong. The owner may also notice excessive discharge coming from the ear. When an ear infection is detected, it should not be ignored. Untreated infections can lead to middle and inner ear infections, which are much more serious and much more difficult to treat.

Elbow Dysplasia

Many different diseases can affect the elbow joint of a Boxer and cause permanent and progressive damage. Often, the first warning an owner has that his or her Boxer has elbow dysplasia is when the dog suddenly can't walk or put weight on his front legs. The elbow joints are hot with inflammation, and arthritis begins its destruction in the joint.

Diagnosis of the disease involves X-raying the dog's elbow joints and sending the X-rays to either the Orthopedic Foundation for Animals (OFA) or Genetic Disease Control in Animals (GDC). Registry numbers are assigned by both organizations to Boxers that are free of disease. In dogs with elbow dysplasia, OFA grades the degree of dysplasia from I (a slight case) to III (full-blown degenerative joint disease). Since elbow dysplasia is thought to be a genetic

disease, Boxers with *any* degree of the disease should not be bred. Though there is no cure for elbow dysplasia, preventive measures—or those things that may help prevent the onset of the disease in a dog who is predisposed to the disease—may include the following: maintaining a healthy body weight (not fat), avoiding excess calcium and protein in developing dogs, and providing easy, regular exercise for young dogs.

Hip Dysplasia

This crippling disease is thought to be genetic. Interestingly, and frustratingly to some breeders, some dogs with hip dysplasia can live their lives without ever showing clinical signs of the disease. The disease for these dogs only appears on an X-ray. Current theory holds that these dogs are predisposed to the disease, but may not have developed symptoms of hip dysplasia because of certain environmental factors.

At any rate, this disease is degenerative, which means that once the cycle of destruction begins in the joint, it is very hard to slow, perhaps unlikely that it can be completely halted, and impossible to reverse. As mentioned above, diagnosis for the disease is by X-ray, which is taken between one year and two years of age, depending on the type of X-ray taken and the registering body. Registration of clear hips is maintained by OFA, GDC, and PennHIP.

Once a dog is determined to be dysplastic, treatment varies with the symptoms of the dog, the dog's age, and the progression and destruction of the disease. Joint supplements and NSAIDs may be used to ease discomfort and lessen inflammation in milder cases. Severe cases of hip dysplasia may require surgery.

Preventive measures include selecting a puppy from a breeder who has registered at least three generations of Boxer hips as free of disease, but this, of course, is not a guarantee of clear hips in the puppy, yet; in the future, it may be. For now, however, puppy owners need to take preventive measures in feeding their Boxer puppies food that meets but does not exceed their nutritional requirements. Nutritional supplements such as calcium, phosphorous, and vitamin D have been shown in studies to exacerbate growth problems. Also, exercise should not be extreme, but rather should be easy and steady, such as jogging and swimming, so that the hip joints do not suffer any trauma. The buildup of muscles around the joint is also believed to be beneficial to the hips in preventing dysplasia.

Hypothyroidism

Any time a Boxer becomes lethargic, his owner should start looking for answers. One reason may be that the Boxer is suffering from hypothyroidism in which thyroid hormones are produced in insufficient quantities. Hair loss is seen in some Boxers suffering from hypothyroidism, but more than half never show this symptom. Some Boxers

may simply be suffering recurrent infections.

The disease is difficult to diagnose, but with the battery of tests now available, if a veterinarian suspects this disease, diagnosis is possible. Treatment is lifelong but is relatively easy—a hormone supplement taken once or twice daily. The only difficulty is that the diagnosis must be accurate and can't be an educated guess because excess thyroid hormones can affect the heart.

Senior Boxer Health Concerns

As an aging dog, the senior Boxer is prone to several different conditions and disorders. The following is a brief summary of those non-life threatening issues that most commonly confront the silver Boxer.

Arthritis: Normal (and abnormal) wear and tear on the joints wears away on the cartilage found on joint surfaces. Once the body's natural cushioning is thin or worn away in places, the joint becomes irritated and becomes inflamed. Ways to help your Boxer to be comfortable include: daily, gentle exercise; maintain a light, fit weight; keeping toenails short; non-slip rugs on slick floors; and comfortable, thickly padded bedding. Veterinary treatment to ease pain may include joint supplements, nonsteroidal anti-inflammatory drugs (NSAIDs), and pain medication.

Cognitive dysfunction syndrome: As dogs age, they can suffer from a loss of cognitive functioning, just as humans do. Symptoms of cognitive dysfunction syndrome (CDS) include disorientation, interrupted sleep cycle, sudden loss or confusion with housetraining, and variances in social behaviors. CDS is treated with prescription medications and therapeutic diets, along with mental stimulation (interactive toys, walks outside, teaching new tricks, etc.).

Gingival hyperplasia: If a Boxer's teeth aren't brushed regularly by you, and cleaned annually by your veterinarian, the gums will gradually envelop the dog's teeth, necessitating surgery. This condition is painful for the Boxer and is almost entirely preventable.

Incontinence: This condition is usually found in spayed, overweight female dogs. Urine leaks when the Boxer is completely relaxed or sleeping. The leak may be small or a flood. When other possible causes are ruled out, an incontinent Boxer will need to be kept at a fit weight (less pressure on the bladder), exercised (strengthens muscles around the urinary sphincter), and possibly put on medication specifically to control incontinence. The medicine is inexpensive and exceptionally effective with few if any side effects. For those Boxers who don't respond to oral prescriptions, collagen injections have been highly effective when used to narrow the urinary sphincter.

Lipomas: Aging dogs can develop fatty tumors, or lipomas. These tumors are benign and usually occur just under the skin, though they can appear in muscle tissue or other areas. Though unsightly, lipomas do not pose any threat to the aging Boxer's health *unless* the tumor is in a position that makes certain movements or relaxed positions uncomfortable. Only then will a veterinarian consider removing the tumor. **Tip:** Because Boxers are prone to mast cell tumors, which can be deadly, make sure every new lump is tested to determine if it is a harmless lipoma or something that requires your veterinarian's immediate attention.

Nuclear sclerosis: This is a natural clouding of the eye and is a normal process of aging. The nuclear sclerosis can gradually reduce a Boxer's vision. Seek veterinary attention if your Boxer shows any signs of pain or discomfort in his eyes.

Pressure calluses and sores: If a Boxer has an arthritic right hip, he may prefer to lie on his left side. If he lies on his left side all the time (and often on hard surfaces), he will develop thick calluses on his left elbow. Though unsightly, this is simply a toughening of the skin where pressure is being put on a regular basis. Keep an eye on the area, however, in case the callus becomes an open sore. If your Boxer develops a pressure sore, seek veterinary care immediately to prevent secondary infections. Also, whether your Boxer is developing calluses or has a sore, seek out ways to make your Boxer's arthritis less painful and his favorite places to lie down more comfortable.

Chapter Twelve

The Well-behaved Boxer

There are many reasons why you should not only make sure your Boxer is trained, but trained well.

1. A Boxer who will sit, stay, lie down, and come when called is a manageable dog. If the dog is consistent in his responses to commands, he becomes a reliable dog. A reliable, manageable Boxer can be taken virtually anywhere with his owner and will be completely controllable. Imagine the places you can take your Boxer knowing that you won't be dragged across the street or have your dog attempt to have a confrontation with every dog that comes within a half-mile radius. You'll also be confident that your Boxer will respond in a friendly manner to everyone you meet *because you've trained him to respond this way.*

2. Your training efforts will help to establish you in the leadership role. When your family is also involved in the Boxer's training, the entire family shifts into this leadership role, too. When the "boss" or "bosses" are accepted by your dog, you generally will have few if any problems with your Boxer attempting to push you or your children around. And if you *do* have problems, if you are attending a training class, your trainer will be able to help you work through these problems.

3. The time you spend with your dog will strengthen the human-animal bond. Yes, your Boxer will love you just because you're you, but he will love you even more—and you will appreciate your Boxer more—if you become active partners. Obedience training is an excellent way to begin this process.

4. The exercise, both mental and physical, that your Boxer will get from being trained is stimulating. The Boxer is a working dog and loves to have a job to do. If there's no job, your Boxer will likely assign himself one to keep from becoming too bored. The only problem with this self-appointed job is it probably is something you'd rather your Boxer *not* do, such as rearrange the furniture or relandscape your backyard. So, give your dog a job and watch him flourish!

5. If you train your Boxer to be a gentleman or lady, you will be more popular. Neighbors will invite you to cookouts, your boss will give you a raise, and—well, maybe training your Boxer won't produce such dramatic results in your social life, but whether your neighbors say it or not, they will appreciate living next to people who care for their dog and who they feel are responsible owners. You may never hear a compliment verbally, but had you not trained your Boxer and had you left him to his wild ways, *you would have heard a lot,* and none of it would have been good.

Teaching the Basics

To get you started, following are the basic commands you will want to begin teaching your puppy or adult. Remember, keep the lessons positive. The trick is to reward and praise your Boxer when you catch him doing something right.

Watch Me

One of the hardest things to achieve with a puppy is to get him to pay attention to you for more than a nanosecond. Sometimes it seems that it's hard just to get the puppy to recognize that you've said his name (maybe he doesn't know his name!). To get your Boxer to begin recognizing that he needs to watch you when you say his name, begin playing the *watch me* game. This works for adult Boxers who are new to training, too.

Take a nice fragrant treat, such as hot dogs cut into little pieces, bits of

broiled chicken breast, or beef jerky, and, holding it in your fingertips, put it close enough under your Boxer's nose to get his attention. Bring the morsel up under your chin and say, *"Watch me,"* or the dog's name, *"Elvis!"* When the dog looks at you, immediately reward him with the treat. As the puppy or dog gets the hang of the game, you can hold the treat under your chin and move around a bit. Feel free to act silly; your Boxer will love the show. Reward the Boxer for watching you. You will notice that your Boxer will quickly focus on you whenever you give him the *watch me* command or say his name.

If you're home during the day, perform this exercise intermittently throughout the day; you will want to walk around with a hip pack filled with prechopped treats. If you work away from the home, try this exercise in the morning, after you get home, and intermittently until you retire for the night. Keep it fun and praise, praise, praise when your Boxer does it right.

Sit

This command may be the most helpful behavior you ever teach your Boxer. A dog who bolts out that door can be put on a *sit*. A growing puppy who wants to jump up and grab the food bowl out of your hands can be put on a *sit* until the food is set on the floor. A *sit* prevents a boisterous Boxer from jumping up on unsuspecting visitors. The *sit* is also a simple exercise to teach your dog.

Put a treat in your hand and wrap your fingers around it. While holding your Boxer gently by the collar, pass the hand with the treat slowly from the dog's nose to the top of his skull. As the dog shifts his weight to track the treat, he naturally sits. As your Boxer completes his fold into a *sit*, say, "Sit!" Do not say the command unless you are absolutely sure he is going to *sit*. In fact, it is fine to practice with the treat, rewarding him for a *sit*, and not use the verbal command until he is folding into the *sit* position quickly and eagerly. The key here is to link the verbal command with the action of sitting. Timing is everything! After you've rewarded him for sitting with praise and the treat, release him with an exuberant release command, such as *"OK!"*

With a little practice, your Boxer soon will be eagerly sitting every time you say, *"Sit."* In the early stages, *always* reward with a treat, and with lots of enthusiastic praise.

Sit-Stay

This is the *sit* command with an added bonus—a *stay*. Once your dog is sitting consistently with the *sit* command, you can begin adding the *stay*. Attach a leash to your dog's collar and put him in a *sit*. Now, give your dog the *"Stay"* command (verbally) along with the *stay* command (visually). The visual command for the *"stay"* is either a right-to-left short sweep of the hand in front of the dog's nose, or simply the hand in front of the nose. Once you have verbally told your dog to stay, take one step to the right, leaving your left leg next to your Boxer. Rock your weight to the right and then immediately shift to your left leg and return your right leg to its original position. Good *stay!* Reward your dog quietly with praise and a treat. Repeat this exercise so he is used to you shifting your weight away from him and then returning. Next, give him the *stay* command and hand signal, and step to the right, allowing your left leg to follow so you are standing one full step away from your Boxer. Pause a second and step back to your dog. Continue in (literally) small steps, gradually increasing your distance and time away from your Boxer.

Down

The *down* command is a natural progression from the *sit,* so you'll want to make sure your puppy or adult understands the concept of sitting on command. The *down* command is particularly good to use when you are going to be somewhere with your Boxer and you want him to be comfortable, but you also want him to be in control. The *down* position is a more submissive position for a dog and can be used to help reinforce the handler's leadership. Dogs are also less likely to bark in the *down* position, so this command also has its usefulness with barking Boxers.

To teach the *down,* put your Boxer in a *sit.* Then, while gently holding the dog's collar, take the treat and slowly move it from the dog's nose down to the ground. If your Boxer is steady in his *sit,* he will naturally move to a *down.* If he is less steady in his *sit,* he may try to pop up his haunches and rock forward to retrieve the treat. If this happens, put your Boxer back in a *sit*

and repeat the exercise. Eventually, the *down* will become a regular part of your dog's repertoire, too.

Remember, don't worry about adding the verbal command for *down* until your Boxer is fluidly following the treat and moving swiftly and easily from a *sit* to a *down* position. Once your Boxer understands what you want him to do, then you can link the word *"down"* when he is in finishing his *down*.

Down-Stay

The *down-stay* is taught in the same manner as described for the *sit-stay* except the Boxer begins the *stay* in the *down* position. As your dog becomes more reliable on his *stays,* begin moving a little distance away from him, always keeping him on a leash. Using a recall leash—30 ft. (9 m)—begin varying the distances you move from your dog during the *down* and *sit-stays.* Again, never take your dog off the training leash; never give him a chance to fail. Once

your dog can be trusted at a distance, increase the time at which you stay at the end of the long leash.

Stand-Stay

The *stand-stay,* which is very convenient for veterinary exams and grooming, is taught in the same way as the *sit-stay* and *down-stay,* except the dog is, of course, standing. With your Boxer standing on your left side, first give the command *"Stand,"* and then the command *"Stay."* Just as with the *sit-stay* (page 170), you'll want to take one step out and immediately step back, giving your Boxer as little chance as possible to fail. Increase the distance and time away very, very gradually.

Come

The recall command, when heeded, saves lives. No matter how careful an owner is, there is always that one instance in which your Boxer slips away and heads straight for the road. If you've taught your Boxer the recall command, your chances of him turning and coming back or perhaps just stopping are far greater than if you have not trained your Boxer at all.

With puppies and with adults, the recall command can begin as a game. If you have several family members or friends who enjoy your Boxer, have them sit in a large circle in a fenced yard. One at a time, take turns calling the Boxer to you. Anything goes. Get down on the ground. Clap your hands. Act silly, but do whatever it takes. When the Boxer comes, say "*Come!*" and give him lots of love; praise him wildly. Then have another member in the circle do the same thing. Pretty soon, the Boxer will associate coming as something good.

When your Boxer has mastered the *sit-stay,* you can perform this exercise solo. Put the Boxer on a *sit-stay,* walk out to perhaps five feet (1.5 m) on the recall leash, and call your dog. Praise him enthusiastically for coming. Keep working at greater distances until your Boxer literally can gain enough speed to bowl you over. If he does, don't worry; you can think about adding another *sit* command on the end of the recall later. For now, you want that enthusiasm and you want a speedy and reliable recall. It may just save your Boxer's life someday.

Walk Nicely

If there's one thing that Boxers *aren't* known for, it's nice walking

manners. Invariably, you'll see a 65-lb. (29-kg) hulking male Boxer dragging his owner around the block, going wherever he pleases. Why? Because when the Boxer is a puppy he naturally follows his owners around. It's also easy to exercise a puppy in a small area, such as a backyard, so a leash isn't needed. But walking puppies on leashes is *very* important if you want to have control later.

As soon as you get your puppy home, you can begin working on the *walk nicely* exercise. Basically, the exercise requires that you use your voice to keep the Boxer puppy close to you. If the puppy strains on the leash, stop and use your voice to bring the puppy back into you. No pops or jerks are necessary in this exercise. Just lots of attention and a few treats. Change directions gently and encourage the puppy to stay with you, too. Work on this exercise several times a day, every day, and your Boxer will catch on quickly. Gradually, you can work this exercise into heeling, in which the Boxer must stay at your side, looking up at you attentively as he trots.

The Art of House-training

A good training chapter wouldn't be complete without a section on the most rudimentary of training basics: house-training. Fortunately for Boxer owners, the breed tends to be very fastidious when it comes to hygiene. Boxers don't like to lie in or near their urine or waste, which works to the owner's advantage. The key is to set your puppy or adult up for success and minimize his chances for failure.

When a Dog Needs to "Go"

In addition to first thing in the morning and last thing at night, there are several times your Boxer will need to relieve himself during the day: after exuberant play, after eating, immediately upon exiting the crate, and, if he's a puppy, every two hours while he's awake. You're now thinking, "Is there any time this dog *doesn't* have to 'go'?" If you want to house-train your Boxer quickly with few to no mistakes, the answer is, "In the beginning it's better to be safe than to be investing money in steam cleaners and spot removers."

Crate Training

The use of a crate is one of the fastest ways to train your dog that outside is where the "potty" is and inside is strictly off limits. As mentioned earlier, the Boxer doesn't like to be dirty. If the dog is left in a room by himself, he can happily run behind the couch and relieve himself there, but if the Boxer is in a crate, he has nowhere to go, so he won't unless he really has to.

Your job is to predict when your Boxer will need to go and to walk him or take him outside. Follow your Boxer and when he finds a spot, praise him gently *while he is in the act of relieving himself.* You may feel a little silly following your dog around the yard, but the praise works. Remember, catch him in the act of something good and reward him. You can even give the dog a treat right after he has relieved himself in the correct place.

House-training takes consistency (always allow the dog to relieve himself regularly) and positive reinforcement (praise and treats). Also, never give your Boxer too much freedom too soon. Take baby steps. The Boxer must associate that (1) the crate is home and he mustn't dirty the crate, (2) the room in which the crate is housed is home and this area mustn't be soiled either, and (3) all the rooms in this wonderful home are "inside" and they are all off limits! This association is very gradual for puppies. Adult dogs may make the association much faster, but still don't allow them to fail.

Mistakes Will Happen

You just walked your Boxer, he relieved himself, and you brought him inside to enjoy a few minutes with you in the newly carpeted family room. A few seconds later, you discover that your Boxer left you a present. Take two steps back in the house-training game. What do you do?

If you discover the mistake after the fact, do nothing. Do *not* yell at your Boxer and definitely do *not* physically correct him. Your Boxer thinks in the present and will associate any verbal or physical correction with his current behavior: "Hey, I was lying nicely in my bed and you just came in and scolded me." Shame on you. Instead, get your cleanup supplies and take care of the mess.

The time to correct your puppy is when he is *in the act.* If you catch your puppy as he is relieving himself, pick up the puppy and say, *"Ah-Ah!"* Rush the puppy out to the yard, place him in a suitable spot and praise him gently when he does the right thing. Give him a treat, clean up the mess inside, and forget about it. Do remember, however, to keep a closer eye on your dog the next time.

Potty Commands

Yes, you can teach your Boxer to relieve himself on command. Every time you take your dog outside specifically to relieve himself, say *"Go potty,"* or some other related code that only you and your Boxer will know. Repeat this command several times every time your puppy or dog relieves himself. Soon, you will be able to take your dog out and give him the *potty* command, and your Boxer will start looking for a spot.

Why would you want to teach your dog this type of command? If you travel with your dog, you will immediately know why. Rest stops can be few and far between. When you find one, you can't be picky. If your dog is used to relieving himself only on mulched beds or on closely cropped grass, he may be uncomfortable in other locations. Still, if you've trained him to relieve himself on command, he will try to go anywhere. *Go potty* is an extremely helpful command and a real time-saver, too.

Other House-training Tools

Dog doors: Dog doors can be a tremendous convenience. The flexible door is set into a storm door, allowing the dog to go in and out at will. This door can be a great way to facilitate house-training with young dogs because it allows the Boxer to relieve himself when he needs to, not just when you're around. The door must open into a fenced backyard on one side, and into a protected area of the house on the other. Ideal locations for dog doors are in washrooms that exit into the yard on one

side. If gated into the washroom, there's not much for the Boxer to destroy. A hard, scrubbable floor is also a prerequisite for the room inside the dog door.

Pitfalls of dog doors are that the Boxer must learn to use it and not abuse it, considering that it could be seen as a fun chew toy. Also, although the door gives your dog more freedom during times when you're not home, it also allows your dog more freedom to bark at dogs on the other side of the fence, and drag things into your home, including mud, mulch, and plants he didn't like in the flower bed.

Pet gates: Another product that can facilitate house-training is the pet gate. If your dog is out of his crate, pet gates are a must for keeping him exactly where you want him, but don't count on them for total safety. The crate is the only way you will know that your Boxer is where he is supposed to be. Gates can be climbed and a determined Boxer can pull these devices from the walls. If your Boxer seems to respect the gates, great; you're one of the lucky ones. Just don't count on these products as fail-proof.

The key to successful house-training—and any form of training for that matter—is to be consistent, remain positive, and reward and praise your Boxer when he does the *right* thing. He truly wants to please you. You just have to be able to teach him what you want him to do. In the end, your patience and dedication will pay off.

Chapter Thirteen

When Good Boxers Behave Badly

No dog, not even a Boxer, is perfect all of the time. Usually, every dog possesses at least one or two habits that can drive an owner crazy unless something is done to control the situation. This chapter will cover the basic problems good Boxers sometimes display, the reasons behind these behaviors, and some solutions. Most dog behaviors can be worked through given a little perseverance, patience, and creativity on the part of the owner.

Common Behavior Problems

The following behaviors are those that can be seen in many Boxers, particularly those who are left to their own devices during the day or night to keep busy. Often, the simplest solution is to give the dog a job and keep him busy. Unfortunately, because of many owners' working schedules, the simplest solution is not always the easiest. Few dog owners can spend 20 or more hours a day with their dogs unless they have a home-based business—or unless the dogs *are* their business.

The following are some suggestions to help owners assist their dogs in overcoming what could develop into bad habits.

Barking

Boxers are not known to be "barky" dogs; they typically sound the alert and then quickly settle down when the "all's well" sign is given by the owner. There are always exceptions to the rule, however, or those Boxers who feel it is their duty to be both day watchman and night sentry.

One solution is to bring the dog inside. Sounds simplistic, but it works. If a dog is outside, he is bored. He is also stimulated by all sorts of sounds. If he feels a particular sound is strange, unfamiliar, or threatening, he will begin barking until the threat is gone or the noise has silenced. Of course, these heroics are not admired by your neighbors under whose window your dog is barking. With the dog inside, he is no longer stimulated by the sounds and he settles in for the night.

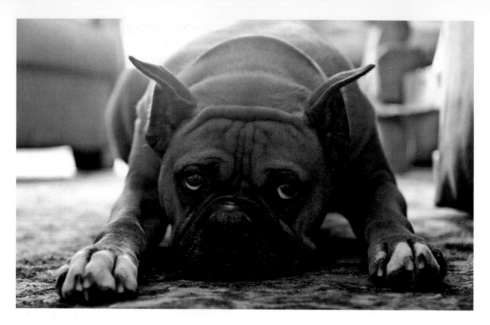

But what if you have a dog door and your dog runs in and out all day for every little sound and you're at the office and can't monitor your dog's activities? This one is tougher because the dog is serving as a watchdog, which you want him to do. What you don't want is incessant barking of a dog who likes to bark just to hear his own bark.

Spray collars can be quite effective in training a dog not to bark. Every time the dog barks, he is sprayed with a bad-tasting but harmless solution. Some dogs, however, figure the collar out and purposely bark until the liquid is gone so they can bark away at their leisure. Another option might be to consider using an electronic stimulation collar at a very low setting. This type of collar must be used only when the owner is home and can monitor the dog's activities. Also, because the collar can deliver a jolt to such a shorthaired breed as the Boxer, great care needs to be taken not to abuse the collar.

Digging

Dogs dig for many different reasons. Sometimes digging trenches just seems like a lot of fun to a Boxer. Other days, when it is warm outside, a big hole in the ground would provide a nice cool spot to snooze. Then there are Boxers who bury their bones and are perpetually digging them back up. And there are still other Boxers who will burrow a tunnel to escape under the fence.

The answer to the bored dog is, of course, either to keep him occupied and with the owner, or confined to an area where he can't get in trouble when the owner isn't looking.

The dog who is digging for a cooler place needs to be kept inside on warm days or provided a shady, breezy spot in the yard for limited time periods. Owners of dogs who enjoy digging have had some success with designating a digging patch in their yards for the dog and even burying items for their dogs to uncover. Another solution might be to install a partial underground electric fence that limits the Boxer's activities to one area of the yard, or to build a kennel run for the dog to use when the owner cannot be in the yard to supervise where and when the dog is digging.

For the Boxer who is digging his way under the fence, determine why he has such an intense desire to leave his home. If the Boxer is a male, neutering will calm the "call of the wild" and will help to keep your wayward male at home. Spaying will also help a female Boxer from attracting all the neighborhood dogs from digging under your fence, and will serve to take her drive away for meeting up with would-be dog suitors.

Is Your Boxer Getting Enough Exercise?

This is an incredibly athletic breed that craves mental and physical exercise. Regular training will help with some of the mental needs of the Boxer, but good, regular exercise twice a day with your Boxer will go far in helping to satisfy his energy needs. Many Boxers who are exhibiting undesirable behaviors simply need more exercise. The saying is definitely true: a tired Boxer is a *good* Boxer.

Chewing

Mostly a problem with teething puppies, destructive chewing is best controlled by providing your Boxer plenty of safe chew bones and toys. If the dog still can't be trusted, or if he has a particular liking for sixteenth-century antiques, it will be necessary to keep the dog and his teeth away from anything you don't want reconfigured. This can be accomplished with judiciously crating the dog when you can't watch him, or by confining him to an area of the home in which there's nothing of value that can be destroyed.

Nipping

Sometimes puppies will jump up and nip at children's clothing, limbs, and such. This is a puppy game that must be nipped in the bud. Puppies who nip children or their owners are looking at their human family as equals—in this case, as puppies. This association must be stopped so that the dog realizes that he is on the bottom of the totem pole in the house. This is achieved by involving your children in training the dog. Very young children can sit in a parent's lap and give the dog a treat after he obeys a command given by the parent. If the nipping and rough play accelerates because your children won't listen to you and persist in screaming and running and jumping around, encouraging this rough play, then separate the children from the Boxer and vice versa. Once the

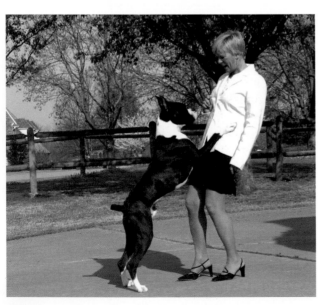

puppy progresses through the teething stage, the primary time for nipping and chewing on children, you may find the situation settles down substantially. If not, continue training your Boxer and your children to respect each other, and separate children from dogs when you cannot give them your undivided attention.

Jumping Up

Boxers are enthusiastic, good-hearted dogs who love their people. And what better way to show their favorite humans just how much they love them than by jumping up and wrapping their forelegs around them? Bam! The only problem is that even a medium-weight Boxer is capable of tumbling a sturdy, unsuspecting individual.

The best way to discourage this exuberant greeting is to teach your Boxer the *sit-stay.* When introducing your dog to strangers or friends, put the dog in a *sit-stay* and require the dog to remain in this position when greeting people. With this training tip a lot fewer people will be bowled over. Of course, getting your Boxer to *sit-stay* when *you* come home may be a bit more difficult.

Jumping Over

Boxers are an athletic breed and leaping over the backyard fence may be a piece of cake for the determined Boxer. This leaping or climbing ability is a good way to wind up with a lost or stolen Boxer. To squelch the incidences of fence climbing, the owner needs to take a look at why the dog wants to get over the fence. Is the dog bored? Is he left out alone in the backyard for hours on end? (A big "no-no" with a Boxer.) Does he need more exercise? If so, then a good daily romp with his favorite person may be all this fence jumper needs to stay home.

The problem could also be that you have an intact male Boxer in search of a female in season. Neutering will solve this problem, but if the dog has already learned how to climb the fence, other steps may need to be taken to insure the safety of the dog.

First of all, is the fence high enough? It should be at least 6 ft. (1.8 m) tall. Is the fence climbable? Chain-link fences can give dogs a foothold, whereas a solid privacy fence is flat and slick. In severe cases of fence jumping, the fence may have to be constructed with a slightly inward slope. Or a hidden electric fence could be used around the base of the fence. And finally, the dog could be allowed an exercise run with a roof to prevent future escapes.

Separation Anxiety

Separation anxiety is usually experienced by a puppy when he first arrives at his new owner's home. Everything is new and strange and the puppy misses the warmth and security of his mother and littermates. Of course, he quickly overcomes this anxiety when he realizes just how much fun it is to live with people.

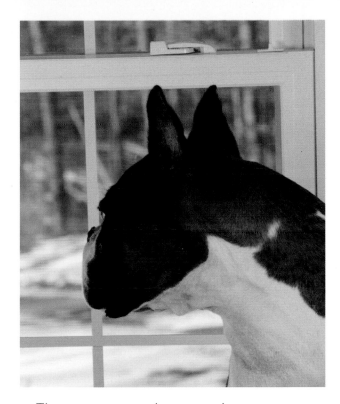

There are cases, however, in which the separation anxiety continues into the dog's adulthood. Whenever the owner leaves the home, the dog goes wild with almost outright terror. Excessive panting, howling, crying, pacing, and elimination are all behaviors the Boxer might exhibit. Some cases of separation anxiety can be so severe that crating alone is not enough to prevent the dog from injuring himself.

Some cases of separation anxiety can be calmed by determining the triggering stimuli for the behavior and providing a new consequence. In other words, if every time you open the front door, you leave, then practice opening the front door without leaving.

Pick up your keys and put them down. Grab your jacket and then hang it back up. Your Boxer knows all your pre-leaving habits and anticipates your leaving. You can diffuse his separation anxiety by disassociating these leaving behaviors with actually leaving. Also, make sure he's good and tired before you *do* leave.

Additionally, there are prescription medications available that have been approved for treating a dog with separation anxiety *but* they need to be used with a desensitization program. One of the best programs is detailed by Patricia McConnell in her book *I'll Be Home Soon* (McConnell Publishing, Ltd.: June 2000). Boxer rescue organizations frequently work with separation anxiety issues in rescued adult dogs; a call to a rescue in your area may be able to provide you with an experienced Boxer trainer who can help you and your Boxer work through his issues.

A Special Case: The Deaf Dog

The deaf Boxer is not a problem dog but he does present a different training scenario. Since the deaf Boxer can't hear, you must be able to get his attention in a way other than by using your voice. This means you must cross his line of vision using an object, such as a ball or a beam of light. Deaf Boxers can also be trained to look at their owners when given a pagerlike buzz from an electronic collar or similar device.

The key is to get the dog's attention. Once this is achieved, the dog can be trained with hand signals using the same positive reward training methods as those used for hearing dogs. Treats are critical to get the dog's attention, and consistency in hand signals is also key. Many owners of deaf dogs use American Sign Language, but any form of signals that are easily seen can be used.

Owners who have trained deaf Boxers say they feel the deaf Boxer is actually in some ways more attentive than his hearing counterparts. Because the dog cannot hear, he depends on his owner for some guidance. Some deaf dog owners relate that their dogs are so focused on their hands that the dogs attempt to interpret what their owners are saying when they are actually just "talking" with their hands to a friend.

For more information on training deaf dogs, see Useful Addresses and Literature, page 194.

Chapter Fourteen

Beyond Basics: Getting Involved

Looking for something to do with your Boxer? There are at least a dozen activities you can become involved in with your dog. The Boxer is such a talented, agile breed, and is so eager and willing to work with his owner, it would be a shame *not* to become involved in a sport.

Following are summaries of both competitive and noncompetitive activities that welcome Boxers.

Competitive Activities for Boxers

In competitive events, you and your Boxer will be competing against other dog-human partnerships. Since there are placements—some dog must win—there is competition. In many of these sports, however, the competition is congenial and competitors support each other's efforts. Which sport you choose to participate in largely depends on your Boxer's talents and your dedication to training your dog.

Agility

Agility is the fastest-growing dog sport in the United States. It has literally taken the country by storm. Competitors relate that in many areas of the country, some of the fiercest competition is just in getting registered for an event. Sometimes the only way to assure registration in an event is to overnight-mail the entry so it arrives on the opening day for registration.

There is a reason for the booming popularity of this sport: It's fun. Training schools, which are popping up all over the country, relate that most people begin agility classes just to have fun with their dogs. Pretty soon, they're hooked, and off they go into the world of competition.

Agility is modeled after the equine open jumping classes in which horse and rider are required to complete a course of obstacles in the fastest time with the fewest number of faults. In this case, faults are refusals to jump, poles knocked down, a foot in the water jump, and so on. In agility, the dog must navigate through a series of obstacles, too. Under the direction of his owner, the Boxer must jump over hurdles, weave through poles, slide through tunnels, and trot over a teeter-totter. The dog with the fastest time through the course with the fewest faults is the winner.

In order to compete in agility, the Boxer must be physically mature (older than at least one year), fit, and have no orthopedic problems, such as elbow or hip dysplasia. The dog should also know the basic commands: *sit, down, stay, come.* Dogs of all athletic ability will have fun in this event; the truly agile and keen dogs will excel. Even shy dogs do well in this sport. Working in agility with a fearful dog produces a much more confident companion.

Organizations that sanction agility competitions include the American Kennel Club (AKC), Canine Performance Events, Inc. (CPE), North American Dog Agility Council (NADAC), United Kennel Club (UKC), and the United States Dog Agility

Association (USDAA) (see Useful Addresses and Literature, page 193).

To find an agility training club, ask your local obedience club for referrals. If the local club doesn't have agility courses, they will know who in the area does.

Conformation

Dog showing is truly a favorite hobby among dog fanciers. Dogs are judged against each other in order to find a Winners Dog and Winners Bitch. Points toward a conformation championship are awarded for the top male or top female in the breed at the show on a given day. Obviously, with the numbers of Boxers being shown today, it is very difficult to win and it takes a very well-put-together Boxer to win in the show ring.

Once winners are found from the nonchampion males and females, the winning dogs are then shown against the specials. The specials are dogs who have already achieved their championships. From this class, a Best of Breed and Best of Opposite Sex are chosen. Though this moment is extremely exciting, it isn't over yet. The BOB from the Boxer class then goes on to compete against BOBs from all other breeds from the working group. Including the Boxer, the working group is composed of 21 breeds, including Rottweilers, Doberman Pinschers, Great Danes, and Samoyeds.

When a group winner has been selected, he then waits for the final class: Best in Show. Here the winners from sporting, hound, working, terrier, toy, nonsporting, and herding groups compete for the ultimate award, a BIS (Best in Show).

It takes more than owning a drop-dead gorgeous Boxer to win in the breed ring; it also takes a dog with a

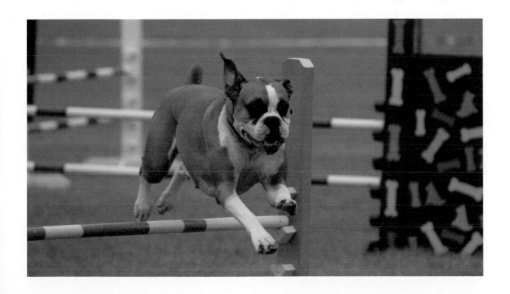

tremendous temperament and movement. And the handler must know how to show off his or her dog to his best advantage. Because of the breed's popularity and the immense sizes of some classes, a person can own a great dog and be a skilled handler but find it difficult to "finish" a dog's championship. Often, in these cases, an owner will consider hiring a professional handler to show a Boxer.

If you decide to show your dog yourself, there are usually classes that you can take at a local obedience club in show handling. These people will give you the tips and instruction you will need to present your Boxer. If you truly have a magnificent dog, you will be able to succeed in the show ring. It may take a little longer if you do it yourself and it won't be inexpensive traveling to all those shows, but the final rewards will be all yours and your Boxer's.

The most recognized sanctioning organization for conformation events is the AKC; however, the UKC also offers shows and championships (see Useful Addresses and Literature, page 193). Additionally, up-to-date information on upcoming shows, entries, and past winners can be accessed at *www.infodog.com.*

Flyball

This sport must have been designed with Boxers in mind. It involves running, jumping over hurdles, catching tennis balls, and getting a little wild. If you have an energetic Boxer who has quick speed and is adept at catching tennis balls, you might really enjoy this sport.

Flyball consists of teams of four dogs and their handlers. It's a relay race in which the fastest team wins. The first dog is sent out to retrieve the flyball. He jumps over a series of hurdles, reaches the box in which the balls are contained, and steps on the trigger that releases the balls. The ball pops up in the air, the dog catches it, and races back to the team where the next dog and handler are ready to go.

To compete in flyball, your Boxer must be healthy and must enjoy being around other dogs. The competitions get noisy and both fans and participants are very keyed up. The sanctioning organization is the North American Flyball Association (NAFA) (see Useful Addresses and Literature, page 193).

Musical Canine Freestyle

Modeled after an equine dressage class that requires riders to perform dressage movements with their horses in sync with music, musical canine freestyle is a relatively new sport that began as a demonstration in Canada. Musical canine freestyle involves complex, rapid maneuvers by the dog and handler choreographed to music. Owners and dogs are often in costume.

Classes include on lead, off lead, single dog and handler, and multidog and handler. If you ever get a chance to see this class, do it. Musical canine freestyle is always a showstopper and pulls the largest audience of all at shows. To become adept at the sport takes a lot of work, according to handlers, and an enthusiastic dog. Because of the Boxer's agility, intelligence, and great physique, he has the potential to be a top performer in this sport. Of course, the owner must be willing to be seen in public, dancing with his or her dog!

Organizations that sanction canine freestyle include The Canine Freestyle Federation, The World Canine Freestyle Organization, and The Musical Dog Sport Association (see Useful Addresses and Literature, page 193).

Obedience

Your Boxer doesn't need to have picture-perfect conformation to become an Obedience champion; he just needs to have an eagerness to learn, a willingness to please, and an owner who can accept the challenges of training such an intelligent dog. The American Kennel Club offers five titles in obedience competitions: Companion Dog (CD), Companion Dog Excellent (CDX), Utility Dog (UD), and Utility Dog Excellent (UDX). The Obedience Trial Championship (OTCh) title is awarded to dogs who have earned a UD and have earned 100 points. Points are tallied according to dogs defeated in classes, placement, and so on. There is also a National Obedience Championship competition that is run once a year by the National Obedience Association.

The AKC also offers "nonregular" classes in obedience, such as the brace class in which two dogs of the same breed are shown unattached or coupled, veterans' class for dogs aged seven or older, and the team class made up of teams of four dogs and handlers.

In the regular classes, each title requires three passing scores or "legs" to achieve that level's title. To be awarded a CD, for example, a Boxer must receive a passing score in three separate trials. Exercises that are required for the entry level obedience class (CD) are:
• heel on leash and figure eight
• stand for examination
• heel free
• recall
• long *sit*
• long *down.*

To receive a qualifying score in the Open class (CDX), the Boxer must successfully complete the following exercises:
• heel free and figure eight
• drop on recall
• retrieve on flat
• retrieve over high jump
• broad jump
• long *sit*
• long *down.*

Utility requirements are a step harder from the Open class:
• signal exercise
• scent discrimination (article 1)
• scent discrimination (article 2)
• directed retrieve
• moving stand and examination
• directed jumping

To excel in obedience, it is wise to find a good obedience club early on in your training. A positive attitude is a must to keep your Boxer enthusiastic about his training!

Both the AKC and the UKC sanction obedience trials. For more information, see Useful Addresses and Literature, page 193.

Schutzhund

Schutzhund is not a dangerous sport for dangerous dogs. Quite to the contrary, a Boxer will do well in this sport only if he is extremely intelligent and possesses great mental soundness. Aggressive, flighty, or unstable dogs will not be able to pass even the most basic level of these tests.

Schutzhund is not all protection work, as some people may think. It is really a test of the versatility of the working dog. In other words, the protection test is only a part of the entire Schutzhund test. In fact, before a dog can even be tested at the first level of Schutzhund work, which includes tracking and obedience as well as protection work, the dog must pass an obedience test and earn his companion dog title: Begleithund (BH).

Schutzhund titles that can be earned include BH or ("companion dog"), Sch.A, Sch.I, Sch.II, and Sch.III. It is important when training for Schutzhund work to find a good working club that has experience with Boxers, if possible. The United States Boxer Association is a national club developed to meet the needs of the working Boxer. The association and its members are very helpful in directing Boxer owners to training information. The association also holds its own Schutzhund trials on an annual basis. For information, contact the United States Boxer Association (see Useful Addresses and Literature, page 193).

Tracking

Boxers are noted for their scenting abilities. Historically, they have been used as tracking dogs and more recently as drug dogs who must locate illegal drugs. In other words, even if your Boxer comes from generations of show dogs and hasn't been asked to track anything, odds are that your dog will still perform well in this sport.

The American Kennel Club offers three levels of tracking: Tracking Dog (TD), Tracking Dog Excellent (TDX), and Variable Surface Training (VST). A Boxer who achieves all three titles is awarded a tracking championship. The tests are pass/fail and are not competitive.

The TD requires a dog to track a fresh scent through turns to find a scented article. The TDX level takes the dog and handler through a more difficult course of varied—and many times physically challenging—terrain. The scent is older, the trail is longer, and there are physical obsta-

cles, such as water and fallen logs. The final test offered by the AKC is the VST, which was designed to simulate a realistic tracking of a person. The test requires that the dog track a scent over both vegetative and man-made surfaces.

To find a tracking club, your first call should be to the local obedience club. Many times these clubs have a subset of members who are actively involved in tracking. For more information on tracking, contact the American Kennel Club.

Noncompetitive Activities for Boxers

In addition to the competitive activities sponsored by a variety of organizations, there are several noncompetitive activities that are well suited for the Boxer.

Backpacking

If you are an outdoors person and are thinking of taking your Boxer along with you on day hikes and perhaps even an overnight trip, you can. As long as your Boxer is not suffering from any health problems and is in good shape, he can be conditioned to carry a backpack with much of his own supplies. There are now companies that manufacture backpacks specifically designed for dogs, so a comfortable fit is possible.

Conditioning your Boxer to his pack is necessary and should be done gradually. Dogs in good shape can generally carry 10 to 15 percent of their body weight in the pack. Exceptionally muscular Boxers may be able to carry as much as 25 percent, but don't push it. Precautions to take when hiking with your Boxer include applying a topical dose of flea and tick preventive prior to your trip, keeping the Boxer on a leash (retractable or recall leashes allow your Boxer to explore safely), and keeping an eye on the temperature. As noted, Boxers do not do well in warm or cold weather, so your best hiking seasons will most likely be spring and fall.

Canine Good Citizen

Do you want to prove that your Boxer is a model canine citizen but you aren't interested in the competitive nature of obedience trials? You may be interested in the AKC's Canine Good Citizen (CGC) Program. The CGC was developed by the AKC to encourage dog owners to teach their canines good manners, both in the home and in public. Many therapy organizations require their dog-human partners to pass the test as a prerequisite to therapy work.

The CGC is a pass/fail test that examines the dog and owner at several levels. To achieve CGC certification, the dog must be presented as a well-groomed dog. He must be willing to approach a stranger and sit quietly as the stranger pets him. The dog must show that he can walk nicely on a leash, walk through a crowd of people on a loose leash,

and perform the basic commands, *sit, down, stay,* and *come.* The dog also must be able to behave well around other dogs.

For more information on the CGC program or for a complete set of test rules, an information kit, and a schedule of testing locations and dates, contact the American Kennel Club, Canine Good Citizen Program.

Carting/Drafting/Driving

The Boxer can pull his weight. If your Boxer is healthy and in good condition, you may enjoy teaching him to pull a small cart. (The famous Friederun von Miram-Stockmann is pictured in an historic photo in which she is driving a small carriage that is being pulled by four of her Boxers.)

The terms carting, drafting, and driving have similar meanings when it comes to dog power and all can be performed by Boxers. Carting involves pulling a wheeled vehicle with or without a rider. Drafting is pulling with no passenger, but perhaps a small load. Driving involves the dog pulling a cart and following the commands of the driver of the cart.

Additional terms of the sport include a cart, which is a two-wheeled vehicle; a wagon, which has four wheels; and a travois, which has no wheels and is a sort of sled used to drag loads containing various items. The two-wheeled cart is the lightest and easiest vehicle to maneuver and is perhaps most suited to the Boxer, which is much smaller in size than many breeds that participate in this sport.

Necessary equipment will include a harness that is comfortable and fits your dog well. You will also need a cart; there are companies that specialize in carting equipment for dogs. Experienced carters recommend waiting until your Boxer is fully developed and mature, which would mean no pulling before the age of 18 months, perhaps even two years.

For more information on carting, the following books and videos are available: *An Introduction to Canine Carting with Beth Ostrander* is a 60-minute video illustrating basic carting, use of the equipment, and training techniques (available through *Dog Works* at http://www.dogworks.com/books/bkdraft.htm); *Newfoundland Draft Work* by Consie Powell (also available through *Dog Works*); and *Draft Equipment Guide* by Roger Powell (also available through *Dog Works*).

Rally

Are you interested in obedience but aren't quite ready to take such a formal plunge into the training world? The non-competitive sport of Rally may be just for you. Unlike formal obedience, the handler is allowed to talk to his or her dog throughout the test. It's very similar to a real training situation—and *Rally is fun!*

In a Rally event, a series of "stations" are set up in a standard size ring. The stations are numbered (so you don't get lost going through the course) and each station asks you to do something with your dog. One station could be "Halt-Sit." The next station could be "360-degree Left Turn," followed by another station labeled "Fast Pace." At the Novice or entry level of Rally, the dog and handler will be given a course that includes 10 to 15 stations. Every event is set up differently (with different exercises and a different order), so the clever dogs (who tend to figure out what is happening "next" in the Novice levels of obedience), never know what is going to happen next. And, because the handler is allowed to verbally praise and talk to his or her dog, the enthusiasm is never squashed in this sport!

Organizations that offer rally events include the AKC, the Association of Pet Dog Trainers, and the United Kennel Club (see listings under "Organizations," page 193).

Community Service Activities

Pet therapy: There are many benefits of dog ownership. According to various studies, dog owners tend to be happier, healthier, and live longer. Why not share some of the Boxer love with a person who is less fortunate than you? If you have a Boxer who is well trained and is not easily rattled by an accidental ear pulling, he may have what it takes to become a therapy dog or a pet visitor.

Therapy dogs are canines who are incorporated into a health care facility's care plans. In other words, the visits made by the dogs and handlers are part of the patient's therapy program and are used to make specific gains in the patient's progress. With pet visitation, the dog's visits are made to brighten up the spirits of the facility's residents, as well as add some spontaneity to the schedules of the staff. Both forms of therapy are equally rewarding, and the difference in them can be a matter of how the facility approaches and incorporates the visits into its overall programing.

For a dog to become a therapy dog, he generally must possess his Canine Good Citizen certification (see page 190), and be certified by a recognized animal assisted therapy (AAT) association. Certification by the AAT association often requires a temperament test and the completion of and graduation from an AAT program.

One AAT organization is the Delta Society (see Useful Addresses and Literature for contact information). This organization provides home study kits, as well as a plethora of information brochures, pamphlets, articles, and other materials. Another organization is Therapy Dogs International, Inc.

Search and rescue: Though limited in hot or extremely cold weather, the Boxer can be trained for search and rescue (SAR) work. This work involves tracking over both old and new trails in real-life situations. Though SAR volunteers relate that in some areas of the country the major-

ity of searches are for Alzheimer patients who have wandered off, other searches include lost children, missing adults, and the recovery of a deceased individual. Though civilian SAR volunteers are used only in non-violent situations—murder searches are performed by law enforcement agents—the work can become dangerous. It has been known to happen that a lost person turned out to be murdered, with the murderer still close by.

SAR is virtually a full-time, unpaid volunteer job. Members of local SAR teams must be available to leave at a moment's notice and travel, sometimes to distant or even international locations. Once in the field, the dog-human team must be able to survive in the wilderness on its own for 24 hours. Training is also rigorous for both dog and owner, but SAR volunteers would have it no other way.

This activity is certainly exciting and will tax both your dog's and your physical and mental stamina. It is also a deeply rewarding activity. To find an SAR team in your area, volunteers suggest contacting your local law enforcement agency to find out with whom they work. Other people who might know who to contact would include members of your local obedience club. SAR units affiliated with the American Rescue Dog Association (ARDA) can be located by accessing the association's web page or writing to the association (see Useful Addresses and Literature for contact information).

Useful Addresses and Literature

Organizations

Breed Information

American Boxer Club
www.americanboxerclub.org

American Kennel Club
8051 Arco Corporate Drive,
   Suite 100
Raleigh, NC 27617-3390
(919) 233-9767
www.akc.org

German Boxer Klub
Boxer-Klub E.V. Sitz München
Veldener Str 64+66
81241 Munich, Germany
011 49-89-546708-0

United Kennel Club
100 E. Kilgore Road
Kalamazoo, MI 49002-5584
(269) 343-9020
www.ukc.dogs

United States Boxer Association
www.usabox.org

Agility

American Kennel Club (AKC)
See listing under "Breed Information."

Canine Performance Events, Inc.
   (CPE)
P.O. Box 805
South Lyon, MI 48178
www.k9cpe.com

North American Dog Agility Council
P.O. Box 1206
Colbert, OK 74733
www.nadac.com

United Kennel Club (UKC)
See listing under "Breed Information."

United States Dog Agility
   Association
P.O. Box 850955
Richardson, TX 75085
(972) 487-2200
www.usdaa.com

Behavior

Animal Behavior Society
2611 East 10th Street, Office 170
Indiana University
Bloomington, IN 47408-2603
(812) 856-5541
www.animalbehavior.org/ABS

American College of Veterinary
   Behaviorists (ACVB)
A listing of all current Diplomates
from the ACVB are listed on
the organization's website:
www.dacvb.com

American Veterinary Medical
   Association
1931 N. Meacham Road, Suite 100
Schaumburg, IL 60173-4360
(847) 925-8070
www.avma.org

Association of Pet Dog Trainers
   (APDT)
150 Executive Center Drive, Box 35
Greenville, SC 29615
(800) PET-DOGS
www.apdt.com

International Association
   of Canine Professionals
P.O. Box 560156
Montverde, FL 34756-0156
(877) THE-IACP
www.dogpro.org

National Association of Dog
   Obedience Instructors (NADOI)
PMB 369
729 Grapevine Hwy
Hurst, TX 76054-2085
www.nadoi.org

Boxer Rescue
American Boxer Rescue Association
P.O. Box 184
Carmel, IN 46082
www.americanboxerrescue.org

Search and Rescue
American Rescue Dog Association
P.O. Box 613
Bristow, VA 20136
www.ardainc.org

National Association for Search
   and Rescue, Inc.
Education Services Director:
   Janet Adere
(703) 222-6277
www.nasar.org

Deaf Dogs
Deaf Dog Education Action Fund
P.O. Box 2840
Oneco, FL 34264-2840
www.deafdogs.org

Freestyle
Canine Freestyle Federation, Inc.
www.canine-freestyle.org

Musical Dog Sport Association
515 S. Fry Road
PMB # 301
Katy, TX 77450-9100
www.musicaldogsport.org

The World Canine Freestyle
   Organization
P.O. Box 350122
Brooklyn, NY 11235
(718) 332-8336
www.worldcaninefreestyle.org

Schutzhund
United Schutzhund Clubs of
   America
3810 Paule Avenue
St. Louis, MO 63125
(314) 638-9686

United States Boxer Association
See listing under "Breed Information."

Therapy Dogs
The Delta Society
289 Perimeter Road East
Renton, WA 98055-1329
1-800-869-6898
www.deltasociety.com

Therapy Dogs International, Inc.
88 Bartley Road
Flanders, NJ 07836
(973) 252-9800
www.tdi_dog.org

Books
Art: Secord, William. *Dog Painting, 1840–1940, A Social History of the Dog in Art.* Suffolk, England: Antique Collector's Club, 2003.

Secord, Willliam. *A Breed Apart: The Art Collections of the American Kennel Club and The American Kennel Club Museum of The Dog.* Suffolk, England: Antique Collector's Club, 2001.

Blind Dogs: Levin, Caroline D., R.N. *Living with Blind Dogs*. Oregon City, OR: Lantern Publications, 2003.

Massage: Fox, Michael W. *The Healing Touch for Dogs.* New York: Newmarket Press, 2004.

Tellington-Jones, Linda. *Getting in Touch with Your Dog.* Roxbury, ME: Kenilworth Press Ltd, 2006.

Activities
Agility: Canova, Ali, Diane Goodspeed, Joe Canova, and Bruce Curtis. *Agility Training for You and Your Dog: From Backyard Fun to High-Performance Training*. Guilford, CT: Globe Pequot Press, 2008.

Simmons-Moake, Jane. *Agility Training, the Fun Sport for All Dogs.* New York: Howell Book House, 1992.

Simmons-Moake, Jane. *Excelling at Dog Agility: Book 1: Obstacle Training*. Houston, TX: Flashpaws Productions, 1999.

Animal-assisted Therapy: Burch, Mary R. *Wanted! Animal Volunteers.* New York: John Wiley & Sons, Inc., 2002.

Burch, Mary R., and Aaron Honori Katcher. *Volunteering with Your Pet: How to Get Involved in Animal-Assisted Therapy with Any Kind of Pet.* New York: John Wiley & Sons, Inc., 1996.

Howie, Ann R., Mary Burch, and Ellen Shay. *The Pet Partners Team Training Course: Pets Helping People Manual*. Seattle, WA: Delta Society, 2001.

Canine Good Citizen: Volhard, Jack, and Wendy Volhard. *The Canine Good Citizen: Every Dog Can Be One*, 2nd Edition. New York: John Wiley & Sons, Inc., 1997.

Conformation: Coile, D. Caroline. *Show Me! A Dog Showing Primer*, 2nd Edition. Hauppauge, NY: Barron's Educational Series, 2009.

Flyball: Olson, Lonnie. *Flyball Racing: The Dog Sport for Everyone.* New York: John Wiley & Sons, Inc., 1997.

Obedience: Anderson, Bobbie. *Building Blocks for Performance*. Crawford, CO: Alpine Publications, 2002.

Bauman, Diane L. *Beyond Basic Dog Training*. New York: John Wiley & Sons, 2003.

Spector, Morgan. *Clicker Training for Obedience: Shaping Top Performance Positively*. Waltham, MA: Sunshine Books, Inc., 1999.

Rally: Dennison, Pamela S. *Click Your Way to Rally Obedience*. Crawford, CO: Alpine Publications, Inc., 2006.

Kramer, Charles "Bud." *Rally-O: The Style of Rally Obedience,* 3rd Edition. Manhattan, KS: Fancee Publications, 2005.

Search and Rescue: Judah, J.C. *Building a Basic Foundation for Search and Rescue Dog Training*. Morrisville, N.C.: Lulu Publishing, 2007.

Tracking: Krause, Carolyn. *Try Tracking! The Puppy Tracking Primer*. Wenatchee, WA: Dogwise Publishing, 2005.

Behavior/Training

General Dog Behavior: Aloff, Brenda. *Canine Body Language, A Photographic Guide*. Wenatchee, WA: Dogwise Publishing, 2005.

Bailey, Jon S., PhD. and Mary R. Burch. *How Dogs Learn*. New York: John Wiley & Sons, Inc., 1999.

Donaldson, Jean. *Oh Behave! Dogs from Pavlov to Premack to Pinker*. Wenatchee, WA: Dogwise Publishing, 2008.

McConnell, Patricia B., PhD. *For the Love of a Dog: Understanding Emotion in You and Your Best Friend*. New York: Random House Publishing, 2006.

Behavior (Problem): Donaldson, Jean. *Mine! A Guide to Resource Guarding in Dogs*. San Francisco, CA: Kinship Communications/ SF-SPCA, 2002.

Killion, Jane. *When Pigs Fly: Training Success with Impossible Dogs*. Wenatchee, WA: Dogwise Publishing, 2007.

McConnell, Patricia B., PhD. *I'll Be Home Soon! How to Prevent and Treat Separation Anxiety*. Black Earth, WI: Dog's Best Friend, Ltd., 2000.

McConnell, Patricia B., PhD. *The Cautious Canine: How to Help Dogs Conquer Their Fears*. Black Earth, WI: Dog's Best Friend, Ltd., 1998.

McConnell, Patricia B., PhD. and Karen B. London, PhD. *The Feisty Fido: Help for the Leash-Aggressive Dog*. Black Earth, WI: Dog's Best Friend, Ltd., 2003.

Pryor, Karen. *Don't Shoot the Dog! The New Art of Teaching and Training.* Waltham, MA: Sunshine Books, Inc., 2006.

Rugass, Turid. *Barking: The Sound of a Language*. Wenatchee, WA: Dogwise Publishing, 2008.

Rugass, Turid. *My Dog Pulls. What Do I Do?* Wenatchee, WA: Dogwise Publishing, 2005.

Clicker Training: Book, Mandy, and Cheryl Smith. *Quick Clicks: 40 Fast and Fun Behaviors to Train with a Clicker*. Wenatchee, WA: Dogwise Publishing, 2001.

Pryor, Karen. *Click! Dog Training System*. (Book and clicker.) New York: Metro Books, 2007.

House-training: Palika, Liz. *The Pocket Idiot's Guide to House-training Your Dog.* New York: Penguin Group (USA), 2007.

Socializing with Dogs: Bennett, Robin, and Susan Briggs. *Off-leash Dog Play: A Complete Guide to Safety and Fun*. Wood-bridge, VA: C&R Publishing, LLC, 2008.

McConnell, Patricia B. *Feeling Out-numbered? How to Manage and Enjoy Your Multi-dog Household* (expanded and updated edition). Black Earth, WI: Dog's Best Friend, Ltd., 2008.

Socializing with People: Long, Lorie. *A Dog Who's Always Welcome: Assistance and Therapy Dog Trainers Teach You How to Socialize and Train Your Companion Dog.* New York: John Wiley & Sons, Inc., 2008.

McConnell, Patricia B. *How to Be the Leader of the Pack and Have Your Dog Love You for It!* Black Earth, WI: Dog's Best Friend, Limited, 1996.

Magazines and Websites

The Boxer Ring
P.O. Box 128
Edwardsville, IL 62025
(618) 960-6316
www.theboxerring.com

Boxer Underground (A bi-monthly Internet magazine)
www.boxerunderground.com

Boxer World (informative website)
www.boxerworld.com

Deaf Dog Mailing List
http://pets.group.yahoo.com/group/ deafdogs

Index